AF689198

FEMINISTS NEGOTIATE THE STATE

The Politics of Domestic Violence

Edited by

Cynthia R. Daniels

with

Rachelle Brooks
Paris De Soto
Elizabeth Felter
Sandra Marshall
Laurie Naranch
Anne Sparks

University Press of America,® Inc.
Lanham • New York • Oxford

Copyright © 1997 by
University Press of America,® Inc.
4720 Boston Way
Lanham, Maryland 20706

12 Hid's Copse Rd.
Cummor Hill, Oxford OX2 9JJ

All rights reserved
Printed in the United States of America
British Library Cataloguing in Publication Information Available

Library of Congress Cataloging-in-Publication Data

Feminists negotiate the state : the politics of domestic violence /
Cynthia R. Daniels, Editor ; with Rachelle Brooks . . . (et al.).
p. cm.
1. Wife abuse--United States. 2. Abused women--Legal status,
laws, etc.--United States. 3. United States. Violence Against
Women Act of 1994. 4. Battered woman syndrome. 5. Feminism--
United States. I. Daniels, Cynthia R. II. Brooks, Rachelle.
HV6626.2.F46 1997 362.82'92'0973--dc21 97-30132 CIP

ISBN 0-7618-0883-3 (cloth: alk. ppr.)
ISBN 0-7618-0884-1 (pbk: alk. ppr.)

™The paper used in this publication meets the minimum
requirements of American National Standard for information
Sciences—Permanence of Paper for Printed Library Materials,
ANSI Z39.48—1984

Dedicated to the memory of

Mae Papastamos

Contents

Foreword

I grew up in a house where my father's violence against me was an accepted part of daily living. My mother's one concession to this occurrence was to close the windows so the neighbors would not hear my screams. I have never been easily controlled, and my father's violence was clearly an effort to obtain such control. At 17, I escaped, going to live with my married cousin and her family. My cousin and her husband were supers in an apartment building. They offered me an empty room in the basement as a refuge in exchange for babysitting. As the mother of a six month old and an eighteen month old, only nineteen herself, she desperately needed the help and I, being employed in a fast food restaurant, desperately needed the free room. The sense of relief I felt was overwhelming, but it was not to last. Not long after moving in, I was awakened by screams. I opened my door to my cousin, babies in tow, running from her apartment. We wound up barricaded in my room for the rest of the night. When the pounding on the door subsided, and the babies fell asleep, she confided the extent of the violence she had been subjected to over the past years. I begged her to leave, to go somewhere safe. She had nowhere to go, she said. It was 1974, there was no place to go.

In the ensuing twenty or so years, I have been involved in the battered women's movement in some way, sometimes as a volunteer, sometimes as a staff member in a shelter program. I have talked with women on the hotline; met them in court, and in emergency rooms with crying children hiding behind huge plastic garbage bags that contain all that they have been able to salvage. I have heard tales of unspeakable horror and cruelty. I have wrestled, along with other activists, with the brutal truth that women are not safe anywhere, even in shelters, following two rapes that occurred at knife point within the shelter. I have seen women so battered and bruised that there was no place on their bodies to put a comforting hand without inflicting further pain. I have watched women frantically try to get housing before their shelter time was up. I have helped women pack up to go back, carefully reviewing safety plans, respecting their decision, but silently wondering if their partners will kill them the next time. Because they do, although it is true that women are most at risk when they try to end the relationship.

On a glorious April morning, one year ago, as I stood in my driveway packing the car for a trip, I heard my neighbor, Alison, scream. I froze. More screams, three funny sounding pops, breaking glass, then silence. On her front step, thirty minutes after our daughters had left for school, the abusive boyfriend whose relationship she had severed the previous day, ended her life.

In the past twenty years everything has changed and nothing has changed. These are the voices I carry with me. I have only to close my eyes to hear Alison's screams. Finally, there is someplace to go, a refuge exists, but it cannot keep women safe or even alive. Yesterday morning, almost a year after Alison's murder, in the next town, a young woman was shot to death by her boyfriend, two days after she ended the relationship. On Thursday, he sent her roses, the paper said. On Friday, he killed her....

Darlene Furey
April, 1995

Introduction
The Paradoxes of State Power

Cynthia Daniels

> Between 1959 and 1975, 58,000 U.S. soldiers were killed in Vietnam. During that same period, 51,000 women in the U.S. were murdered by male partners. (New Jersey State Department of Community Affairs, Division on Women, 1994)

> A man in one of our batterer programs asked whether the government that wanted him to stop his violence was the same one that had trained him to kill in Vietnam. (Stark 1993, 658)

Over the past twenty years, feminists have won critical and significant political victories on the issue of domestic violence. The state has legitimated, legislated, and enforced policies that protect and empower women. Funding for battered women's shelters, better training for police officers and judges, legal rights in the courts—all of these are signs of the success of feminist activism on domestic violence.

Yet the state has failed to address the deeper sources of domestic violence and in many ways helps to perpetuate the masculine culture of violence which helps to produce it. As mandatory arrest policies illustrate, a state empowered to protect women may also have power to victimize women. Many victories won by feminists, like the Battered Woman's Syndrome defense for women who murder their abusers, have been won at the expense of reinforcing traditional patriarchal assumptions that women are unable or unwilling to take care of themselves. In addition, while the state funds battered women's shelters, it has failed to provide women with the economic resources needed for their long-term empowerment.

As feminists demand government action to address gender inequality they are confronted by the paradox of state power—a state which both promises women protection, but protects the interests of men. Using domestic violence against women as a case study, our purpose is to examine the trade-offs and compromises faced by feminists in this process of negotiating with the state. We examine, in particular, feminist engagements with each of the three branches of government, looking in detail at the actions of the Executive branch (through mandatory police arrest policies), the Judicial branch (through the use of Battered Woman's Syndrome in the courts) and the Legislative branch (through analysis of the Violence Against Women Act). Feminist accomplishments, in each of these cases, have been tempered by losses—losses which often drop out of the political system the needs and interests of women who have the greatest need of state resources.

In the United States, domestic violence against women is recognized as an enormous problem. Over the last two decades, police departments, courts, and legislatures have made significant efforts to address this problem. For example, many police officers as well as judges and potential jurists must go through sensitivity training which addresses the sex bias inherent in the U.S. criminal law system. In addition, Congress has passed the Violence Against Women Act which provides over one billion dollars in violence prevention programs. Across the political spectrum, domestic violence is now recognized as an issue which demands state response. It is the shape and nature of this response which we examine here.

Despite feminist victories in winning support for women in the courts and shelters, domestic violence against women has only *increased* since the 1970s. According to one major study, while the violent crime rate for male victims has decreased since 1973, the rate of violent crimes against women remained consistent from 1973 to 1991. In 1991 over two and one-half million women were violently assaulted—twenty-eight per cent at the hands of their current or former partners (Bachman 1994, 1). According to FBI statistics, almost one-third of all women murdered are murdered by husbands or boyfriends. This was true in 1971 (Roberts 1981, 6) in 1986 (Center for Women Policy Studies 1991, 4), and 1994 (Bachman 1994, 1). Every year, four thousand women are killed by abusive husbands or partners (Bachman 1994, 1). Each year, more than one million women seek medical assistance for injuries caused by battering. In fact, a woman is more likely to be assaulted, injured, raped or killed by a male partner than any other type of assailant (New Jersey State Department of Community Affairs, 1994; Belluck 1997). According to recent U.S. Department of Justice figures, half of all women will experience physical abuse from a spouse or partner in her lifetime (quoted in Buchwald 1993, 249).

We use the term "domestic violence against women" to distinguish violence directed towards *women* from child and elder abuse. We reject non-gendered terms such as "spouse abuse" because these terms obfuscate criticism of the traditional patriarchal family. Furthermore, we use the term "domestic" to refer to a present or *past* intimate relationship. As Evan Stark observes, "The vast majority of battered women (75% or more) are single, separated, or divorced, with separated and divorced women facing the greatest risk of severe ongoing violence, including homicide" (Stark 1993, 667). We acknowledge that using the term "domestic" connotes traditional gender roles in the nuclear family; however, we use the term more inclusively to address violence in non-traditional intimate relationships as well.

We approach domestic violence against women from a variety of perspectives. We first outline the history of the state's involvement with the problem of domestic violence against women in Chapter One. Tracing the colonial period to the present, we describe the various forms that women's approaches to the state have taken. Here, we emphasize that domestic violence has been culturally and politically constructed; moreover, domestic violence has been a socio-political concern of women activists for over one hundred years, decades before a recognizable feminist movement emerged.

In Chapter Two, we examine the power to name domestic violence against women. We explore the history of terminology used to define the issue—from "wife abuse" to "family violence" and discuss the reasons why the language we use to describe social problems is so important. We also frame domestic violence as an issue of citizenship grounded in the right to bodily integrity which links private violence with public restitution from the state.

Reflecting the structure of the U.S. government, we next examine executive, judicial, and legislative responses to domestic violence against women. Chapter Three discusses the interaction among the police, feminists, and those affected by domestic violence. The effects of police action differ dramatically, depending upon the race, class, and sexual orientation of the women and men involved in domestic abuse.

In Chapter Four, we outline the emergence and effectiveness of Battered Woman's Syndrome as a defense in court cases. That battered women could also be defendants in the courts was not formally recognized until the late 1970s, when it became evident that some women who kill their abusive partners do so out of self-defense. Chapter Five focuses on the Violence Against Women Act, the most significant piece of federal legislation to address the issue of domestic violence against women. The history of the Act is outlined and the difficulty of working with the state through legislation is examined.

Chapter Six assesses the effectiveness of the strategies feminists have used to negotiate the state in efforts to help battered women and to end domestic violence.

Finally, we have included an Appendix as a way to explore feminist theories of the state in more detail, emphasizing the necessity of theoretical clarity regarding the state as a prerequisite for effective feminist action. We suggest the outlines of a theoretical model—the "gendered state" model—which we feel best captures the paradoxical nature of state power.

This book developed out of a group project in an interdisciplinary graduate seminar at Rutgers University and as such represents an intensive collective writing effort. Although each chapter was authored primarily by one member of the working group, each chapter also bears the imprint of many hours of invaluable collective discussion.

Chapter 1

A History of the State's Response to Domestic Violence

Elizabeth Felter

> A spaniel, a woman, and a hickory tree,
> The more ye beat them, the better they be.
> *Old English Proverb*

Our Colonial Heritage and the "Family"

The European settlers who arrived on the shores of colonial America brought cultural norms from Great Britain and Europe with them. The settlers followed complicated Judeo-Christian values and established a judicial system based on English Common Law. How did these norms affect women?

First, many European Christian leaders sanctioned wife beating.[1] Both Old and New Testaments authorize the dominance of men over women (Davidson 1978). For example, the following passage is found in the New Testament: "Wives, submit to your husbands as to the Lord; for the man is the head of the woman, just as Christ is the head of the Church" (Ephesians 5:22–23). Yet, while some Christian theology sanctions male violence against women, its doctrine is complex, sometimes vague, and open to reinterpretation. For example, in the passage immediately following Ephesians 5:23, the author, Paul, admonishes men to love their wives as they love their own bodies.[2] In addition, Christian arguments historically have been used by women's rights advocates of the eighteenth and nineteenth centuries, such as Mary Wollstonecraft and Maria Stewart, to advance the cause of women's equality (see Wollstonecraft [1792]1988; Loewenberg and Bogin 1976).

Second, English Common Law tolerated abusive husbands. Common law in Great Britain accepted wife beating, the most famous ruling being William Blackstone's "rule of thumb": a husband could beat his wife with a rod no thicker than his thumb (Rhode 1989, 238; Davidson 1978, 95; and Okun 1986, 2). However, Terry Davidson points out that English Common Law was more lenient towards women than continental European law in the mid-eighteenth century. Many European countries, such as France, based their codes on Roman civil law (Davidson 1978, 95). Under Roman law, husbands were held responsible for any crime their wives committed. Thus, men were permitted to abuse their wives physically in order to prevent them from committing a crime (Okun 1986, 2). The settlers who established the American colonies brought this complex heritage with them.

The early settlers of Plymouth and Massachusetts Bay considered family a crucial component of their religious "experiment." Persecuted in England, the Puritans who left in search of a better life "hoped that their [newfound] 'city upon a hill' would set an example of religious devotion for the rest of the world." Peaceful families would create the social order necessary to survive in the new world (Pleck 1987, 17). Historian Paula Giddings lends insight into the values the settlers brought with them,

> [The men who colonized the New World] had been shaped by the Renaissance, with its cult of individualism and the "moral" right to exploit those weaker than oneself; by the Protestant Reformation's ethic and evangelical piety, which separated body from soul; by the Age of Discovery, which found a continent of people different from the explorers; and by the Commercial Revolution, with its vision of wealth on a global scale. (1985, 34)

In Puritan Massachusetts, institutions such as the church, the neighborhood, and courts formed the precursor to the modern state. Survival of the community was a daily difficulty, and neighborly surveillance provided protection for victims of family violence. Indeed, the moral code of the Puritans was strict and forced all inhabitants to conform. Puritan clergyman Cotton Mather "preached that for 'a man to Beat his Wife was as bad as any Sacriledge. Any such a Rascal were better buried alive, than show his Head among his Neighbours any more'" (Pleck 1987, 18). This did not mean, however, that women were respected as individuals in the way that men were. While a strict moral code dictated against male violence in the home, women could be accused of witchcraft if they did not conform to their husbands' wishes (19). Just as men who beat their wives were a threat to the Puritans' social order, women viewed as too independent posed a similar threat. Women accused of witchcraft were violently punished or killed (Morgan 1970, 609). Here, the early "state" strictly regulated men's and women's behaviors, but the state punished women's deviations from culturally accepted behaviors more severely.

Ministers and neighbors paid visits to families suspected of being violent. The church court heard the most severe cases, and the congregation decided whether or not to accept the accused's confession. This process was not designed to determine innocence or guilt. The congregation wanted "to wring from the person on trial a confession of sin in the hope of securing for the wayward soul the promise of salvation" (Pleck 1987, 20). Again, women found themselves in a precarious position. When the church court decided cases of rape or wife beating, the congregation preferred to keep the family together rather than to protect the victims (21). Elizabeth Pleck describes early Puritan ideology as an attempt to reinforce and maintain hierarchy:

> The Puritans sided with the weak, the dependent, and the helpless only if they were seen as blameless...Although there were humanitarian and biblical dimensions to the Puritan legal code, the major purpose of their laws was to reinforce hierarchical relationships, either in the family or in society. (1987, 25)

The intersection of slave and free black women with early colonial America's belief in the "sanctity of the family" further exposes the transparency of this ideal. Not only did the early state give men leeway to abuse their families and servants, but the sanctity of the family as it appeared in early legal and political doctrine only applied to white families. Giddings finds records as early as 1619 that categorized women in one of two categories: wives or servants. In 1619, African women were free in the colonies, but soon after 1619, the categories of "wife" and "servant" crystallized along racial lines with the advent of African slavery (Giddings 1985, 34). While the white family was expected to form a unit, with a man and his wife at its center, most slave families were separated. Slave holders sold family members at auctions. Slaves attempted to escape their desperate situations and left their families. And of course untimely and early deaths separated many black families (Davis 1983, 14–15).

In discussing domestic violence, it is important to keep in mind that women (black, immigrant, lower class) who worked in other men's homes were subject to violence and abuse in their employers' realms. In these cases, "domestic" violence occurred outside their own homes, yet still within a private realm out of reach of the legal system. Being employed outside the home did not mean that rules governing such work were more fair or better regulated. For example, nineteenth-century black activist Fannie Barrier Williams observed that for young black women, "an education not only had a dramatic impact on their status and quality of life, but often shielded them from the sexual harassment that many of them confronted in White homes" (Giddings 1985, 101).

A new idea that dramatically affected white women's role in the family emerged in the 18th century: the bourgeois cult of domesticity. European philosophers such as Rousseau and Hegel claimed women's natural roles were domestic: wife, mother, and organizer of the household. They thought that women were inherently inferior to men because of their fragile physiques and weak minds. This exaggerated concept of femininity encompassed contradictory roles for women—they were defined as both sexual creatures and sexless and pure. Women did not belong in the public, masculine realms of business, politics, education, and religion (Riley 1990, 40–41).

In the nineteenth-century United States, this "cult of domesticity" and related ideas of femininity helped shape how social workers responded to wife beating. Early social workers viewed women who reconciled with their abusive husbands as good wives (Gordon 1989, 257). The cult of bourgeois domesticity may have helped white women seeking refuge at the new agencies and organizations aimed at alleviating family crises.[3] Gordon notes that the individuals who worked at such agencies exhibited a "commitment to the bourgeois ideal of domesticity...[that] also predisposed them to taking responsibility for the protection of women" (252). The founders and staff of emerging family service agencies viewed certain women (those of northwest European descent) as needing protection from men. Other women who were abused by their husbands needed counsel and advice on how to run their homes properly.

The Courts and the Law: Leaving Some "Private" Matters Alone

In early America, the government established civil codes in addition to the early church procedures. Again, early law exhibited contradictory tendencies. On the one hand, the colonists wanted to protect women. On the other hand, they did not provide women full protection from their husbands. Massachusetts Bay and Plymouth passed laws against wife beating, the first such laws in the Western world. The Massachusetts *Body of Liberties* of 1641 stated, "Everie marryed woeman shall be free from bodilie correction or stripes by her husband, unlesse it be in his owne defence upon her assault" (quoted in Pleck 1987, 21–22). One has to wonder how often women assaulted their husbands at this time. Perhaps this legislation's ending clause was an escape for men to justify beating their wives; perhaps women were known to fight back. Additionally, some women found protection in the early state. Between 1692 and 1789, the Governor's Council of Massachusetts granted nine battered women divorce from "bed and board" (meaning a legal separation without the right to remarry); one wife in Plymouth Colony was permitted to live separately from her husband, who was required to pay maintenance to her, but only until he "reformed" (24).

Before law can be applied in court, government must create it. State and federal governments make our laws, and many activists focus their energies in this arena. Legislation lays the groundwork for court rulings and serves to legitimate and define certain behaviors as punishable. Activists in the nineteenth and twentieth centuries attempted to convince Congress and state legislatures to pass laws that would alleviate abused women's plight. By making claims that the state should protect women in their families, feminists attempted to raise the costs for men who abused their wives (see Studer 1984, and Tierney 1982 for a discussion of feminist "claims-making" activities). Some laws proposed that abusers be subject to corporal punishment (the whipping post, for example), capital punishment (the death penalty), legal separation and child custody for the mother, and fines. Activists also fought court decisions such as the one Mississippi passed in 1824, which stated: "moderate chastisement [of the wife by the husband] ... would be allowed in order to enforce the salutary restraint of domestic discipline" (Davidson 1978, 102). A North Carolina court reached a similar decision in 1852. It stated that as long as injuries were not permanent (black eyes, bruises, and cuts were permissible), a husband could not be prosecuted for assault and battery (Oppenlander 1981, 387).

Several women were outspoken on these subjects. Between 1868 and 1870, suffragists Elizabeth Cady Stanton and Susan B. Anthony called for the death penalty for rape (Pleck 1987, 65). As activists agitated, and as cultural norms changed, legislators reacted. In 1871, both Massachusetts and Alabama made wife beating illegal (Davidson 1978, 102). But historical precedent was hard to overcome. A decision reached in 1874 in North Carolina read that it was better for the court to ignore violence in the family, as long as abuse between spouses did not lead to permanent injury (103).

Though some states passed laws against wife beating, women fought for more protection and asserted women's rights. Lucy Stone introduced legislation to the Massachusetts legislature three times (1879, 1883, 1891) which would have allowed a wife to file for legal separation at the police station if the police had arrested her husband for criminal assault. All three times her attempts failed (Pleck 1987, 103). Pleck understands her failure as a function of her "radicalness." The efforts that strengthened the family, that did not challenge economic or racial hierarchies, and that did not question women's social and political status succeeded.

Importantly, feminist activists often confounded the causes of domestic violence with poverty. Francis Power Cobbe, a British political crusader, influenced American activism against wife battering. Cobbe argued that several factors caused domestic violence, including the "squalor of working-class living conditions" (Pleck 1987, 103). While working-class living conditions should have been protested, clearly these women activists separated "us" (upper and middle class women who were not victims of wife beating) from "them" (lower class women who were the primary victims) by using such argumentation.

It is also important to remember that very few women activists pointed to inequitable gender relations as the cause of domestic violence. Most activist women shied away from political action that related men's violence to gender inequality. Language about wife beating appeared in other social and political crusades such as Prohibition, the campaign to liberalize divorce laws, and woman suffrage. Temperance activists Amelia Bloomer and Elizabeth Jones, for example, viewed drunkenness as a male habit that encouraged physical abuse towards wives and children (Oppenlander 1981, 391).

In the 1920s, juvenile and family courts were established to hear cases of domestic matters, including wife beating. In these courts, judges could inquire about a couple's personal misunderstandings, without being bound by the accepted legal rules of evidence. These courts' official policies were to mend the family and urge reconciliation wherever possible. Judges often attributed violence in the home to "the sexual and biological problems of women." In other words, if the wife behaved properly, she could prevent the violence (Pleck 1987, 137, 125).

The Social Service Answer to Domestic Violence

Beyond church congregations, court hallways, and Capitol Hill, individually founded organizations attempted to solve social injustices through "services." In an era where the role of government was limited to warfare, commerce, agriculture, and international affairs, social improvement organizations provided aid to individuals. These organizations began as privately run, privately funded groups.

The first social agencies that attempted to deal with family violence—against children—developed in the 1870s. Wealthy men and women founded the Societies for the Prevention of Cruelty to Children, or SPCCs. Linda Gordon's research reveals that SPCCs and similar agencies in the Boston area around this time were almost entirely staffed by "native-born white Protestant [men], while the clients were immigrant or second-generation Catholic [women and children]" (Gordon 1989, 14). It was around this time that immigration from eastern and southern Europe exploded. Xenophobic arguments polarized native born, older stock Americans and the new immigrants, who were depicted as drunk, immoral, dirty, and criminal (see Kraditor 1981, Ch. 6).

While some impetus behind the creation of SPCCs lay in the desire to alleviate children's suffering, "a wealthy, urban elite was also fearful of social disorder and...blamed the immigrant, largely Catholic, poor." Their primary work consisted of threatening and cajoling neglectful parents, not prosecution or law enforcement (Pleck 1987, 70, 86). While they may have provided some protection for certain groups of women and children, SPCCs also functioned as agents of social control.

In Massachusetts, the SPCCs fielded child abuse cases. However, women tried to alleviate their own abuse through SPCCs. Often, mothers presented their interests as the same as their childrens' interests. Women brought complaints of obscene language and lack of financial support rather than physical abuse to agency staff. Gordon says that at a time "when women's best hope was husbands' kindness, because they were economically dependent on marriage, they did not protest violations of their individual rights, but rested their case on their importance as mothers" (Gordon 1989, 258–259).

Moreover, many of the women seeking services from SPCCs did not perceive a right to freedom from violence in the home. According to Gordon, "they spoke of the inevitability of male violence." While many abused women used tactics such as fighting back, running away, embarrassing their husbands in front of others, and calling the police to protect themselves, they understood that "in a patriarchal system there were neither institutions nor concepts defending absolute rights, but rather custom and bargaining." Perhaps these women, more so than their counselors, understood that they could not use the bourgeois ideal of protecting women to alter power relations in the family. Gordon says that only when women felt they could win did they use a concept of "right" when communicating with agents (Gordon 1989, 256–258).

Agents' racism and classism also affected the assessments of women's problems. Gordon notes as an example the record of a girl who made an incest allegation against her father in 1910. The record taker noted that she "was called 'a romancer but not more so than the average foreign born child.'" The records describe black women as primitive and limited. One was described as "not nearly as talkative as many of her race, but apparently truthful" (Gordon 1989, 14). This language and ideology perpetuated the "us and them" mentality whereby the patrons of social service agencies distanced themselves from the problem and from their clients.[4] Beyond the offices of the SPCC, groups such as the Ku Klux Klan were involved in meting out their own justice against wife beaters, as lawmakers and more established white communities worried about a perceived rise in brutish and violent crime (Pleck 1987, 109).

Clearly, the upper and middle class white community had specific ideas about what wife beating was and who its victims were. Even when seeking to gain autonomy through social service organizations, women of color and of lower classes were not able to define "violence" and "family" themselves (Gordon 1990b, 194). The racism and classism of European American culture around the turn of the century shaped the ways in which white upper class individuals conceived of wife beating. Early social workers' explanations of wife beating cannot be separated from the values of the era in which they lived. In turn, their explanations directly affected the state's response to wife beating. Certainly, if wife beating was an individual problem (it was her fault), there was no reason why the government should be involved in alleviating wife abuse. However, the state had reason to express interest in such violence because the social leaders believed wife beating happened in crime-ridden communities and had the potential to upset United States morality.

As the United States entered more fully into the industrial era, its politics expanded as well. The government faced complex problems such as increasing immigration, a growing population, the Spanish-American War and the First World War. Political scientist Stephen Skowronek (1982) describes this transition around the turn of the century as one from a nation of courts and parties to one of national administrative capacities. The state became more interested in regulating such functions as family life, education, and the welfare of its most important citizens. The new governmental capacities presented alternatives for needy people. Yet, because maintaining order was important to leaders within the new expanding state, services upheld gender and race roles, which people had to meet in order to get help.

In other words, population expansion and diversification, capitalism's proliferation, and rising interdependency of First World economies triggered a series of demands by older stock, middle- and upper-class Americans to establish order. Often order meant maintaining a middle-class notion of family unity, in which strict gender roles were paramount. The arguments for securing woman suffrage (especially during 1910-1920) reflected some of this anxiety (DuBois 1978; Kraditor 1981). In a white, Protestant family, an abusive husband and a submissive wife fit gender roles, and so the state ignored wife abuse, ultimately permitting its existence. On the other hand, the racial undertones of order allowed social service groups to continue operating. In a Catholic immigrant family, an abusive situation fit ethnic roles, and the state expressed an interest in halting (or controlling) their behavior.

The Progressive Era (1896-1920) witnessed the replacement of upper-class volunteers with middle-class scientific personnel as the government bureaucracy expanded. These employees continued to set standards for proper family life, believing they were witnessing an "overall weakening of the family." Single-mother families especially disturbed them. They attributed women's difficulties to their lack of education and lack of mental stimulation (Gordon 1989, 21).

During the Depression, abused women faced difficult circumstances. Gordon says that the economic depression "meant working against all centrifugal forces in the family [specifically economic deprivation] at the expense of asking women and children to suppress their own aspirations" (Gordon 1989, 22). Sympathy for the unemployed husband became an excuse for violent behavior. Treatment for families was often economic aid.

The 1940s and 1950s did not improve conditions for battered women. A gender-neutral, scientific language crept into the discourse of domestic violence with terms like "marital discord" and "marital disharmony." Although women specifically named the violence they experienced, social workers encouraged these women to "probe deeper." Gordon cites one case where a woman claimed her husband threw her on the floor. The social worker said that "she did not believe that mother had to accept this from father but that if mother removed the cause for father's doing this, namely mother's excessive drinking, and inability to get along with father, perhaps this would never have happened" (Gordon 1989, 284). Ideas derived from psychoanalysis, developed by Sigmund Freud, also influenced the solutions handed out to women by counseling centers. Freud's followers interpreted his ideas about female masochism to mean that women fantasized about being abused (Pleck 1987, 157). In a lecture delivered in the early 1930s, Freud claimed that "the suppression of women's aggressiveness...favours the development of powerful masochistic impulses...Thus masochism, as people say, is truly feminine" (Freud [1933]1965, 149).

The Emergence of the Battered Women's Movement

Susan Schechter, in her book *Women and Male Violence*, argues that "in the early 1970s, it sometimes seemed as if the issue of battered women came out of nowhere" (1982, 29). The 1970s witnessed changing political and social norms and the emergence of the battered women's movement which publicized the issue of domestic violence so well that it seemed to be a new phenomenon.

The women's liberation movement clearly affected the beginnings of a new consciousness about domestic violence. One of the oldest shelters for women in the United States began in 1971 as a consciousness-raising group. Many of the early leaders envisioned their shelters as a utopian, nonhierarchical, and liberating experience for women. They understood that women's oppression caused their victimization. In other words, the disadvantages women faced in marriage, work, and family life directly contributed to their abuse. Women's liberation was the key to living free of violence (Schechter 1982, 33–34). Generally, battered women's shelters provided safety to abused women and children as well as organizing space for the battered women's movement.

Other groups created more institutional shelters as well. For example, in 1964, Alcoholics Anonymous established a shelter for wives of alcoholics in California, reinforcing the link their turn-of-the-century foremothers made between male drunkenness and abuse. More institutional shelters grew out of the social service sector (Schechter 1982, 34) and survived because they were better able than shelter-movement feminists to compete for scarce funding (Rodriguez 1988, 217).

The battered women's movement provided badly needed emergency services to abused women, but no corresponding movement evolved to institutionalize abusive men. (See Chapter 3 for a discussion of jailing abusive men.) One institution for abusive husbands opened in Britain in 1971. It operated as an adjunct to a Chiswick Women's Aid shelter, and abusive men could meet and live in a separate facility if they wished (Cohen 1992, 162–163). In a recent survey of battered women's agencies and coalitions, the average number of women served annually per agency was 12,065. The average number of men served was 865 (Davis, Hagen, and Early 1994, 699). While programs for men who batter are available, sheltering facilities for men have not proliferated the same way that shelters for women have in the United States. An historical legacy that a scholar traced to the Middle Ages worked against institutionalizing *men* who batter. It seems more natural to shelter women. European Catholic countries, for example, provided shelter for runaway wives as a substitution for divorce (Cohen 1992, 162). Refuges for women "illustrate women's continued dependence in marriage and economic disadvantage whereby they must rely on a man for the basic necessity of accommodation" (Dobash and Dobash 1992, 60).

The battered women's movement involved many different types of feminists—radical, lesbian, Marxist, socialist—and social and legal workers were active. Social service professionals, while still employing older ideologies of family pathology and psychology, were helpful in getting legislation passed, writing grants, and lobbying (Schechter 1982, 50). Some of the movement's goals were to assist women, to challenge male violence, and to change women's position in society (Dobash and Dobash 1992, 29). Generally, the movement did not confront battering behavior directly, but used state institutions such as the courts and legislatures to increase the costs of battering (Dobash and Dobash 1992, 44).

The fragmentary ideologies that women brought to the "new" activism around domestic violence in no way inhibited the growth and expansion of shelters. By 1982, between 300 and 700 shelters existed (Pleck 1987, 190). By 1989, 1200 battered women's programs existed in the United States. They sheltered 300,000 women and children per year (Dobash and Dobash 1992, 70). In the 1970s, the federal government trained and paid half of all shelter employees through the Concentrated Employment and Training Act (CETA). States began taxing marriage licenses to fund shelters. The Social Security Administration provided the largest single source of money for abused families by funding temporary housing for abused and neglected children (Pleck 1987, 190). However, this only scratched the surface for women in abusive situations.

In 1979, fewer than 15 states had passed laws funding shelters; less than half of all shelters received any money at all from the state or national government (Schechter 1982, 83). Federal legislation for funding of battered women's services was introduced in 1977, but it failed. Today, activists are still looking for more money to support women's shelters and continue to push for federal support. (See Chapter 5 for a discussion of the recent effort around the Violence Against Women Act.) Clearly, the government has avoided taking full responsibility for sheltering all the women who have needed it.

Arguably, the most significant organization that grew out of the movement was the National Coalition Against Domestic Violence. Organized in 1978, it provides financial aid to shelters and services, shares information, and supports research. The Coalition also aims to educate the public about domestic violence and supports changes in sex-role expectations for women (Dobash and Dobash 1992, 36). In 1980, it developed an agenda that included fighting racism at every level of the battered women's movement. They also took a public stance against homophobia (51).

The battered women's movement and the shelters that proliferated defy generalization. Perhaps the most complex dynamic is that shelters are dependent on the society which they have been trying to change. Some shelters are more institutional because of financial pressures, yet some shelters have resisted such institutionalization. Elizabeth Pleck notes that a 1981 survey of 127 shelters found that feminists had established fewer than half. She notes that "the more 'radical' shelters, which often included lesbian feminists on their staff, frequently did not survive" (Pleck 1987, 191). Because shelters could not generate their own revenue, they were dependent on external funding. If benefactors (the government, wealthy individuals, corporations) did not approve of the structure or make-up of the shelter staff, they could cease support. Some shelters, however, have been able to maintain a non-hierarchical structure. For example, one shelter in Hawaii pays all its staff the same salary, has few rules and regulations, and is staffed primarily by former battered women. This shelter, despite early attempts by the local county government to replace it with a more conventional social service agency, eventually earned funding from the state, the county, the local United Way, and a few other funding sources (Rodriguez 1988).

Because it relies on state money, the battered women's movement often is forced to meet the state's terms, and women's energies are devoted to clamoring for more money. Susan Schechter talks about the terms entailed in accepting state money. She calls money "the mixed blessing" (1982, 93). While it provides training, salaries, legitimization of the cause, better record keeping, and the ability of shelters to operate continuously without interruptions, it is also a source of controversy. Money creates a split between administration and service, destroys nonhierarchical structures, and facilitates professionalization of the work. The following example illustrates dramatically the external pressures shelters feel to change their mission or structure: One group wished to attain a Community Development Block Grant of $57,500 from the Minnesota Housing Authority (which has an annual budget of $12 million). "The Commissioners (six men and one woman) rejected the proposal because it was 'sexist' in that men would be excluded from using the proposed shelter. The vote was six to one against" (96).

Activist Lois Ahrens experienced a similar shift in a Texas shelter. The move from participatory, consensual organization to a bureaucratic hierarchy occurred when two volunteers became paid staff, the shelter applied for incorporation as a nonprofit, tax-exempt organization, and some radical feminist organizers began devoting their time elsewhere. Board members with little knowledge of the shelter were elected, and eventually the shelter operated as a social service organization, complete with professionals and clients. Ahrens says,

> We know we cannot exist in a service vacuum. In order for a shelter to be effective, we must initiate and maintain working relationships with the police, courts, hospitals, welfare departments, and mental health services. We must also, however, maintain our own organizational integrity (1980, 47).

Clearly, shelters perform an integral role in women's early steps to establishing violence-free lives. For battered women, relief options expanded considerably in the 1970s. However, we need to question the over-reliance on service which many shelters provide, whether by their own choice or not. Statistics compiled by Davis, Hagen & Early (1994) highlight our concerns. In their study of United States battered women's coalitions and services, they found that these services provided counseling, support groups, specialized shelter, hotlines, transportation, and basic emergency services better than employment training, programs for batterers, transitional housing, and safe houses. Counseling services are more available to women than material opportunities that allow women to change their lives with a new job, and permanent, safe housing, for instance. This tradition, as noted earlier, began with the earliest service organizations. Ahrens points out that, rather than serving the best interests of women and supporting the feminist movement, "the shelter movement will [continue to] attract women (and men) who view these services as stepping stones to personal career goals" (1980, 14).

In the battered women's movement, women have engaged in a struggle between accepting the state's parameters and defining their own solutions. Battered women's advocates had to develop strategies to win in the political arena—to get a slice of the funding pie and a piece of lawmakers' attention. At the same time, significant differences emerged between women trying to solve the problem. Many radical feminists felt that women could never find solutions working with the state, while liberal feminists worked hard on legislation and state intervention. Which is the "right" way? Should we demand that the state help women?

What the History of Domestic Violence Against Women Tells Us

Our ever-changing political and social culture restricts the range of politically viable solutions available at any one time. Making demands on the state and developing strategies to win concessions means that women must confine their arguments within certain parameters, or risk being ignored and marginalized. Imagine that after World War II a group of women went to talk to a Member of Congress.[5] They told him that male violence in the home was unacceptable. They argued that the men who returned from fighting in Europe and the Pacific could not break away from their war mentality and were too aggressive towards their wives and children. They asked the Member of Congress to pass a law that would require all veterans to attend mandatory anti-violence training sessions.

Imagine that another group of women came the next day to talk to the Congressman. They, too, were concerned with male violence, but did not articulate their concern the same way as the first group. They also argued that the men who returned from fighting were too violent, but they linked the violence to the high unemployment rate in their neighborhood. They asked the Congressman to create more jobs in the area.

The second group of women would be more likely to succeed precisely because their request would not upset traditional gender roles. Indeed, it would strengthen them by reinforcing traditional definitions of the husband as breadwinner and the wife as dependent. More employment for their husbands would be an acceptable solution. In the post-World War II era, male violence in the home was not considered deviant behavior, and therefore, the Congressman would have been reluctant to focus his energies there. What kind of electoral payoff would this have provided him? It might have been an electoral liability. While change is not impossible, it most often occurs within parameters that maintain masculine bias.

While options for relief change with time, some concepts remain remarkably constant. As this chapter has pointed out, our ideas about class and race have influenced our ideas about domestic violence throughout history and up to the present. In a recent newspaper editorial, an anonymous writer describes waiting in the hospital emergency room after a night of abuse. She is there with another woman. Each has one eye swollen shut.

> Like the woman across from me...I had thrown on a pair of jeans and a shirt. Somehow, though, I must have looked different from the other woman. The child huddled closer to her mother and whispered something. I pretended I didn't, but I heard it. 'Mommy, I didn't know them kind of ladies got beat up.' (*The Baltimore Sun*, 3 July 1994)

The woman with the child was of lower socioeconomic status than the author. The child's observation about the well-off woman reflects continuing notions about who should get beat up, who doesn't get beat up, and whose agony is more culturally accepted or rationalized.

Re-naming the abuse women face by intimate relations as domestic violence has dramatized the issue and legitimized governmental intervention to alleviate such violence. This chapter has summarized the ways that groups, individuals, and the state have conceptualized domestic violence through our history. It is clear that just getting the issue onto the public agenda is not enough to eradicate the violence that women face. How the issues of violence against women are named as well as framed will help to determine how we respond, as a community, to this issue. For example, if domestic violence is viewed as a problem of early childhood socialization where girls are taught to be obedient and boys as competitive, then solutions will be targeted at schools and educators. It is to the importance of this framing that we now turn. In the following chapter, we discuss the implications of the language used to address issues of domestic violence against women.

Chapter 2

Naming and Framing the Issues: Demanding Full Citizenship For Women

Laurie Naranch

> What happens when the lack of a right to property or speech, bodily integrity or sexual conduct, is cojoined with the vulnerability and dependence created by relative social powerlessness and marginalization? (Brown 1995, 121)

The power to name is the power to give voice to a social phenomena or experience—and to have it legitimated. The feminist movement's fight to make the invisible visible, and to make the silent heard when it comes to women's experiences of their own lives continues to be important. As a result of these efforts, no longer is the problem of domestic violence a woman's problem that she must somehow deserve; domestic violence is a problem of social injustice that must be addressed within the public sphere.

Whereas naming involves an analysis of the words we use to create awareness and to address an issue, framing refers to the fundamental assumptions we make when describing an issue like domestic violence. For example, domestic violence could be framed as a health issue since "[b]attering is the single major cause of injury to women, more common than auto accidents, rapes, and muggings combined" and each year more than one million women seek medical care for injuries from battering (New Jersey State Department of Community Affairs, 1994). It could also be framed as an economic issue due to the fact that missed work days caused by domestic violence injuries account for $3–5 billion lost to industry per year (New Jersey State Department of Community Affairs, 1994). While domestic violence is a serious health and economic issue, in this section we frame domestic violence against women as an issue of rights and of citizenship. We need to analyze the role of the state in relation to women as citizens, given that the right to security of person and bodily integrity are fundamental rights secured via the state.

However, the state that is meant to ensure women's right to bodily integrity has all too often legally sanctioned, ignored, or tolerated women's abuse, and continues to do so today. In October 1994, Judge Robert Cahill sentenced Kenneth Peacock to a mere 18 months in jail and 50 hours of community service for shooting his wife in the head several hours after finding her in bed with another man. Cahill said, "I seriously wonder how many married men would have the strength to walk away without inflicting some corporal punishment" (*New York Times* editorial, 22 October 1994). Judge Cahill effectively legitimated wife killing in a case of infidelity, not to mention threatening the security of other women who are beaten or killed not because they are unfaithful, but because the coffee is cold, or the kids are crying, or his socks aren't clean. Why did Peacock get off with 18 months and Patricia Washington, beaten, induced to miscarry, and threatened at gunpoint *by her husband* get sentenced to 30 years for killing him?[1] Why does the right to bodily integrity apply unequally to women and men? Why is more effort made to control the violent actions of women than of men?

These examples illustrate the inequalities women face when trying to secure equal rights and equal treatment before the law. What are the positive and negative aspects of framing the issue of domestic violence in terms of rights? Merely calling upon the language of rights is no simple panacea; nor should domestic violence be isolated from other issues like welfare, abortion, and economic well-being. Still, the right to bodily integrity is a fundamental right and powerful tool to use when arguing for state restitution to domestic violence. However, we must be aware that securing the right to bodily protection through the state apparatus will not ultimately address the divergent ways women are disadvantaged politically, socially, and economically. Focusing on all three areas is necessary to ensure equality through an invigorated notion of bodily integrity. Currently, in terms of state responses to domestic violence against women, we do not see such an enrichment of citizenship.

The remainder of this chapter is divided into two parts and a brief conclusion. Part one will offer a review of other naming possibilities for the violence women face and explain why we rejected these in favor of the phrase domestic violence against women. The formulation domestic violence against women, we believe, is more amendable to an argument which reaffirms women's status as citizens. We hope to suggest why this formulation has some advantages over other claims, like claims that protect mothers, wives, or spouses, which have often served as the symbol under which women's rights have been subsumed to men's. Part two will provide a brief overview of some of the main themes concerning rights and citizenship for women. By framing domestic violence as an issue of citizenship rights, we hope to illuminate some of the broader issues concerning women's rights.

Part One: Language and Identity

As Chapter One explains, domestic violence emerged as an issue demanding public attention in the late 1960s and early 1970s when the feminist movement began to set up shelters for battered women and strongly campaigned against domestic violence under the declaration "We will not be beaten" (Schechter 1982, 1). Since that time a diverse array of historical and contemporary research and literature has emerged about domestic violence—what it is, speculations as to why it occurs, and how it can be prevented or eradicated. The naming of the problem of domestic violence, however, varies considerably, both historically and currently.

In this essay, we utilize the term *domestic violence against women*, arguing that this term captures more completely the problems of systemic violence against women in intimate relationships. Further, this term has contemporary currency given the high visibility of the O. J. Simpson trial and the Violence Against Women Act in the Crime Bill. In light of the current awareness of domestic violence as an enormous social and political problem, we suggest retaining the term with the addition of "against women."[2] Domestic violence against women is defined as any physical, psychological, or emotional abuse by an intimate against his female partner, regardless of whether she is a wife, ex-wife, girlfriend, or friend. "Domestic" refers not only to violence which occurs in the space of the home, but also to violence which occurs within the relationship of two people.

While women sometimes abuse their male partners, we have chosen to focus on violence against women for a variety of reasons. In the United States ninety-five percent of domestic violence victims are women and each year four thousand women die as a result of domestic violence (New Jersey State Department of Community Affairs, 1994). By contrast, only very few women abuse and/or kill their male partners. In light of these statistics, countless stories of women's abuse by male partners, and the plethora of scholarship documenting this phenomena, the gendered nature of the problem must be seen for what it is—men abusing their female partners.

Today there are a variety of terms used to name the horror of domestic violence. These are terms such as "spouse abuse," "wife abuse," "woman abuse," "battered women," "family violence," "partner abuse," "domestic violence," and "violence against women." What are the advantages and disadvantages of using one term over another? Are these terms interchangeable? This section will explore many of these terms which have been used to name the experience of women who have been abused, and of those who survived.

The language through which the experience of violence against women is translated has a profound impact on one's identity, how one is treated by the legal system, and the ways one goes about making public policy. For example, is a woman who has been abused only a "battered woman" or a "victim" and can she have another identity as something other than an object of abuse? In other words, although she was abused in an intimate relationship, does that mean that she ought to be seen and think of herself merely as an object of male aggression? We need to be cautious not to relegate women to the status of pure victim when the point is to augment women's agency to act and control their lives.[3] Michele Bograd notes, women are not just victims of domestic violence who ask for abuse, they are in fact often survivors who are strong and adaptive (1988, 15). Further, Deborah Rhode notes, theories of women's "learned helplessness" or victim status is a double-edged sword, often granting women legitimacy for self-defense pleas and standing in court, but often disempowering women by "obscuring their capacities for resistance" (1989, 242). Rhode also writes that "the challenge remaining is to use explanations of women's 'victimization' in ways which avoid perpetuating that status" (243). This is a goal we wholeheartedly support. We must work to preserve the tension between the status of women as victims of abuse and, in the words of Linda Gordon, as "heroes of their own lives" (Gordon 1989).

The Power to Name

By giving voice to a problem, women gain the power to make a concern publicly visible as a social and political problem, not just as a personal or individual problem. Feminists have referred to this as the power to name a problem (see Dworkin, 1981). Further, naming the problem of domestic violence against women has helped women raise awareness about the widespread nature of domestic violence in intimate and personal relationships.

A variety of feminists have argued that language does not merely reflect experience, but it in fact constructs how we interpret certain experiences and how we think about our identity (see Moi 1985; Spivak 1987). Joan Scott writes that language is a system "through which meaning is constructed and cultural practices organized and by which, accordingly, people represent and understand their world, including who they are and how they relate to others" (1988, 34). This function of language is especially salient with domestic violence to help those abused and those affected make sense of the problem and feel empowered to take action against the violence. According to R. Emerson Dobash and Russell P. Dobash,

> All work on violence begins with some working definition of the problem, including its name. The name begins to create an image of the problem, and employing a language of description further enhances that image. (1992, 109)

Who produces and controls that image is of central concern to feminists.

The terms used to describe the problem of domestic violence do more than just describe, they set the agenda for a course of action, define the policy options, determine the sanctions to be leveled (e.g. prevention programs, therapy, criminal or civil prosecutions) and against whom they should be leveled. Since domestic violence has traditionally been cast as a private problem, this is the first challenge to confront in naming the problem.

Trying Out the Terms

So far we have suggested using the term "domestic violence against women" and framing the reasons for doing so as an issue of rights. There are, however, other ways of naming the crisis of domestic violence. What follows is a brief review of some other possibilities.

Spouse abuse and *wife abuse* are two terms that locate violence squarely within the marriage contract and the private sphere. As stated above, historically once a woman entered into marriage she became the property of her husband, he having legal and social legitimation to punish her as he would a child or apprentice (see Kampmann 1993, 102). The woman was not considered a citizen with the same right to bodily integrity as a man, particularly within the marriage contract. It was the persistence and power of the feminist movement that produced this as a public problem.

However, there are certain assumptions with each term, "spouse abuse" and "wife abuse," that are limiting factors. Both identify violence within the marriage contract, and rightly so. Yet this fails to address violence inflicted on intimates who are ex-wives, girlfriends, ex-girlfriends, and certainly gays and lesbians who cannot enter into a state- recognized marriage. The difference between the words "wife" and "spouse" should also be highlighted. "Wife abuse" signals abuse that a husband inflicts on his wife, and since at present only women are referred to as wives, the gender specific nature of the abuse can be seen. However, the term "spouse" is gender-neutral—it masks who the batterer is and who is the object of the abuse. Both terms posit a heterosexist paradigm of marriage which limits their use value.

To get around these limitations, for example, some authors expand the definition of wife abuse. Michele Bograd defines wife abuse as "the use of physical force by a man against his cohabiting partner" (1988, 12). While this expands the definition of wife abuse there are at least two limitations. First, it implies that the partners must be in a living situation, (i.e., co-habitating), which does not cover abuse when the pair is separated. Second, by retaining the term "wife," the author still retains the legitimacy of the marriage contract. While that may be rhetorically useful in a context where marriage is the socially accepted status of men and women in long term relationships, it continues to reinforce the marriage contract as the most legitimate and hence most horrific site of violence.

Dobash and Dobash highlight some of these problems when they compare "wife" and "woman" abuse. They write,

> Wife abuse implies that the social institution of marriage as well as gender is central, but it has the drawback that it may also imply that violence is only directed at women living in the legal, rather than the social state of marriage. Woman abuse focuses on gender and avoids the problem of assuming legal marriage but, in so doing, loses emphasis upon analytical insight that the social institution of marriage as traditionally structured forms much of the foundation of the problem. (1992, 39)

While we are not providing an explicit critique of the institution of marriage as inherently unjust, we hope that using the term "domestic violence against women" serves to include violence between intimates inside or outside of marriage.

Family violence can refer to a variety of phenomena, ranging from wife abuse to child abuse to elder abuse. The emphasis again on the family serves to obscure the gender specificity of the abuse and to ignore abuse outside the nuclear family. The function of the term family violence obscures the fact that men are most often the source of violence. Susan Schechter saw and predicted the regression of domestic violence policies for women at the federal level during the tenure of President Ronald Reagan. She suggested first, that the fiscal cutbacks would hurt shelters and secondly, that the traditional family values rhetoric would serve to insulate the nuclear family and further mask the violence that husbands may perpetrate against wives (see Schechter 1982, Ch. 12). In a statement read at the Fifth National Conference on Child Abuse and Neglect in April 1981, Schechter, speaking as a representative of the National Coalition Against Domestic Violence, argued against the consolidation of domestic violence against women with child abuse:

> Child abuse and violence against women are different phenomena with different historical roots. A major goal of child protection is to keep the family united, hopefully free from violence. Our goal is to support a woman in creating a violence-free life for herself and her children in whatever ways she chooses. (1981, 324)

Subsuming child abuse and domestic violence against women would further cloud the abuse women endure, and further relegate them to the status of non-persons within the family structure. The term "family violence" could be used in a way which would include extra-marital relations. That is, family need not be aligned with marriage; the term may include separated or divorced couples. However, given the present use of the term, we suggest that the term family violence obscures the issue of violence against women. Further, the rhetoric of "family" in this case often shores up an ideal family life that has often proven brutal for women and ignores violence by intimates outside of marriages.[4]

The term *battered woman* is used as well. The battered women's movement had a profound effect on bringing the problem of domestic violence to public attention and in setting up shelters and safe houses for women and children. Lenore Walker defines a battered woman as

> a woman who is repeatedly subjected to any forceful physical or psychological behavior by a man in order to coerce her to do something he wants her to do without any concern for her rights. Battered women include wives or women in any form of intimate relationships with men...Any woman may find herself in an abusive relationship with a man once. If it occurs a second time, and she

> remains in the situation, she is defined as a battered woman. (1989, xv)

At this juncture, we can see that the definition of a battered woman can include any woman in an intimate relationship. For example, Donna Moore uses the terms battered women, battered wives, battered spouses, and battered partners interchangeably (1979). The problem is of course that the positions of these women are not interchangeable. It matters if one is a wife or a girlfriend in a court of law. Will there be a divorce? Who will get the children? How will the battered woman be portrayed? Will she be portrayed in the same way if she is a wife rather than a lover? While the term "battered woman" clearly does not mince words as to what the problem is, there may be a tendency of the police and the courts to view this woman as simply a victim. Further, seeing the battered woman as victim may reinforce the idea that all women are somehow "beatable" and that this violence is somehow legitimate in society even as steps are being taken to prevent battering.

Violence against women is a broad term that seeks to address social violence against women. This violence is not necessarily restricted to the domestic sphere, it also includes violence women experience on the street, in school, and in the workplace, for example. This perspective posits that women are the victims of violence because they are women. According to the Center for Women's Policy Studies, violence against women fits the criteria as bias motivated hate crime and should be prosecuted under civil not just criminal laws.[5] This means that similar to other hate crimes, violence against individual women affects the lives of women as a group. Abuse in the home would be included in this definition of violence that could be prosecuted as a criminal and civil offense. The shift in legal definition of the crime is that women who suffer abuse, in or out of the home from partners or strangers, could prosecute not just under criminal law, but also under civil law. This would give further legitimacy to the gendered nature of the abuse and more legal avenues to pursue in arguing against domestic violence. This approach to view domestic violence as a civil offense was given considerable attention when it was included in the national Violence Against Women Act.

As mentioned above, the term domestic violence is generally used to refer to violence in the home. It is a gender neutral term that usually refers to abuse against female (possibly male) partners. Some of the problems here are similar to those discussed above about family violence in that these terms obscure the "fact that males are predominately violent toward women and children" (Stordeur and Stille 1989, 19).[6]

While the move to define the problem on a larger scale, both in the private and public realms, may be necessary, the debates around this issue extend this discussion too far for our purposes. We want to focus on the violence that is too often ignored or dismissed because it occurs among intimates and outside of the public eye. For this reason, we utilize a combination of the above terms to focus directly on *domestic violence against women.* As defined above, domestic violence against women is any physical, psychological, or emotional abuse by an intimate against his female partner, who may be a wife, ex-wife, girlfriend or friend.

The advantages of this definition are threefold. One, it is gender specific. By including the tag "against women" we point to the women who are the objects of abuse. Second, "domestic" refers to the home as well as to the intimacy of a relationship. The advantage of doing this is to address violence that occurs within a situation of co-habitation as well as outside of it. Therefore, we can include wives, as well as ex-wives, girlfriends, and friends in our term. Finally, the preposition "against" is meant to convey the movement of violence of which women are the victims, but more importantly, the survivors.

The term, domestic violence against women, is both inclusive and restrictive. We have included women inside and outside of the marriage contract, and have tried to suggest that the scope of the problem affects adolescent girls as well as and older women, poor and wealthy women, women of all races and ethnic groups. It is restrictive in the sense that this is not a term that will encompass child abuse, elder abuse, abuse of male partners, or abuse in gay and lesbian couples.[7] Further, the term does not name the perpetrator of violence as male. While "male violence against female partners" is a more accurate term, and clearly labels the phenomena, it does not carry the cultural currency of "domestic violence." In trying to name the phenomena of violence against women which occurs in many instances and in many situations, both in public and private, we recognize that women's experiences of violence do not fit into the confines of "domestic violence against women." In trying to name the problem, one must also set the boundaries around it recognizing that they are not permanent or timeless, but rather are theoretically and strategically useful, and hopefully the term domestic violence against women will include more than it excludes at this historical moment.

We could advocate the use of terms such as *domestic partner* or *intimate abuse*. In our definition of domestic violence against women both of these terms arose in order to be more inclusive in our category of "abused." Neither term is gender specific or specifically heterosexual for that matter, which is an advantage when addressing violence in heterosexual *and* homosexual couples who fall outside the boundaries of terms like spouse abuse. However, neither term suggests the gendered nature of the power relations at work between partners or intimates which appears to be their most serious limitation for our present work. We have been suggesting that the gender specific nature of abuse be highlighted; *domestic violence against women* simultaneously highlights a system of power whereby men are in a position of control or dominance over women in a variety of diverse and conflicting ways. At this point in time, understanding this disparity between women and men is essential.

Part Two: Citizenship and the Right to Bodily Integrity

The power to name violence is a central political act, and the way in which a claim to restitution or justice for that violence is posed occurs in a specific political context. In the West, and increasingly in international human rights law, women have been claiming their rights to be free from bodily harm.[8] The public/private split is a central feature of modern, Western political theory and politics. Only the public sphere is seen as politically relevant. As many feminists have pointed out, the question of sexual difference is "inseparable from the question of the relationship between the 'private' and the 'public'" (Shanley and Pateman 1991, 3). That is, women are often associated with the private realm of the family, and men with the public realm of politics and paid work, even though the situation has been different for many women and men according to race, ethnicity, and class. Symbolically and practically the private realm has functioned to "keep women in their place." As Adrienne Rich writes,

> Fundamental to women's oppression is the assumption that we as a group belong to the "private" sphere of the home, the hearth, the family, the sexual, the emotional, out of which men emerge as adults to act in the "public" arena of power, the "real" world, and to which they return for mothering, for access to female forms of intimacy, affection, and solace unavailable in the realm of male struggle and competition. (1979, 215)

Because feminist activists have struggled to create a context of legitimacy for women's claims to political representation, protection, and services, the relationship between the public and private spheres has shifted. Women have claimed their rights as citizens, rights denied them in the private sphere of the home and family. This struggle has by no means been simple or complete.

There are two points of central importance: first, private inequality, violence, and degradation of women undermines rights women ought to have as citizens. The rights women do have are enforced and upheld unevenly according to class and race. This is especially evident when it comes to police response as we will see in the next chapter. Second, the category of citizenship is both powerful and inadequate. That is, citizenship is inadequate when it comes to bodily needs in general, and women's bodies in particular (see Daniels 1993; Jones 1990; MacKinnon 1989). Because women have been excluded from the public realm some feminists argue for equality on par with men. However, an argument for equal rights for women—to be treated the same as any rational man—is insufficient to guarantee equality. We believe that a recognition of the gendered nature of citizenship and a reconceptualization of rights and citizenship are necessary in the context of domestic violence against women. To ensure women's rights as citizens, we must also recognize the gendered nature of power.

Many feminists have been attracted to the power of the language of rights as "a potent weapon against traditional obligations, particularly those of family duty or any social status declared 'natural' on the basis of ascriptive characteristics" (Elshtain [1987] 1991; see also Williams 1991).[9] Central to the language of rights is the idea of self-sovereignty, or bodily integrity, that women have the right to control their own bodies and be free from harm.[10] John Stuart Mill wrote in 1859,

> The State, while it respects the liberty of each in what specifically regards himself, is bound to maintain a vigilant control over his exercise of any power which it allows him to possess over others. This obligation is almost entirely disregarded in the case of the family relations...The almost despotic power of husbands over wives needs not be enlarged upon here, because nothing more is needed for the complete removal of the evil than that wives should have the same rights, and should receive the protection of the law in the same manner as all other persons... (116)[11]

The argument that women should have the same rights "as all other persons" -- men -- is an argument made by many feminists who want to include women in the category of citizen. For example, one early feminist document, the Declaration of Sentiments at the 1848 Seneca Falls conference, followed the format of Thomas Jefferson's Declaration of Independence by declaring: "The history of mankind is a history of repeated injuries and usurpations on the part of man toward woman, having the direct object of the establishment of an absolute tyranny over her" (Declaration of Sentiments, in Ruth 1990). In order to address these injuries, the convention delegates turned toward the state to recognize women as full citizens on par with men, at least, that is, white, property-owning men. Notably, one of the "injuries" inflicted on womankind was the role of wife in the marriage contract, where "she is compelled to promise obedience to her husband, he becoming, for all intents and purposes, her master—the law giving him power to deprive her of her liberty, and to administer chastisement" (Declaration of Sentiments). The remedy, the Declaration argued, was to be found in the immediate admission of women "to all the rights and privileges which belong to them as citizens of the United States" (Declaration of Sentiments).

Many feminists point out that although it is important that women be treated in the manner as all other persons, it is not enough merely to posit women in the mold of a public, civic person. That is, even if women achieve equal legal equality, political representation, and economic means to exercise their rights as citizens, "women's membership in the political community will still be less full than men's" (Jones 1990, 782). This is especially the case when it comes to domestic violence. Carol Pateman highlights this tension in liberal theory which suggests that if women are to become full citizens they must act like men. That is, they must be rational, self-sufficient, and able-bodied. This conception of the autonomous, self-mastering individual cannot accommodate a situation of gender violence in intimate relationships because self-mastering individuals ought to just leave, or deal with it without state intervention—not viable options for most women who suffer abuse.

In a different vein, Catharine MacKinnon argues that liberal law is a "medium for making male dominance both invisible and legitimate by adopting the male point of view in law at the same time as it enforces that view on society" (1989, 237). She suggests that if women are devalued socially in relation to men, no supposedly "neutral" language of law will rectify this unequal situation. MacKinnon writes: "The social power of men over women extends through laws that purport to protect women as part of the community" (243). It is the unequal power relation between men and women which silences women and their experiences of violence. As a solution to this situation, MacKinnon sees the law as a positive vehicle for feminist change. She asserts that women have a specific, collective condition based on inequality with men and that social change must be galvanized around this recognition. This emphasis on women's difference from men has some positive explanatory power when it comes to contemporary gender relations, but falls short in terms of explaining the difference among women and their diverse relation to the state.

To argue that women are the same as men ignores the gendered assumptions in the notion of rational citizenship and in society in general. To argue that women are different from men may end up falsely universalizing the differences between and among men and women. However, we do want to maintain that the discourse of citizenship is itself gendered, not neutral, and for women to access the language of rights, the public sphere must be reconstructed. As a strategy for doing so Jean Bethke Elshtain suggests that

> One must refuse to accept the political silencing of women under terms that either take their social position, traditionally a particular, local and concrete one, for granted or label it and move on to other, more "important" matters. One must find out how the female subject in our time sees herself, or would, were she given the opportunity to provide a spoken account of her existence. (1981, 303–304)

Part of the process Elshtain refers to is the creation of a context, or reconstructed public sphere, where women's experiences would be heard, and where their claims to social justice could be adjudicated. The claim that women ought to have the same rights as men and/or specific protection as women is a debate very much alive in feminist theory and practice; we must not overlook the importance of this debate when it concerns violence against women in the private and public realms.[12]

Conclusion: The Importance of Cultural Conditions

When a woman is more likely to die at the hands of her husband or partner than at the hands of a stranger, when she is more likely to be raped or assaulted at home than in the street, then it is clear that something must be done. We must call this crisis what it is: domestic violence against women. Furthermore, feminists and all affected by domestic violence, must approach the state for action and must create viable resource opportunities for women who are both victims and survivors. This course of action is by no means easy, inherently progressive, or unproblematic. State intervention into issues of domestic violence against women may be necessary, but it is a double-edged sword. We must frame this crisis in the following way: state power and citizenship simultaneously empowers and disempowers women.

Moreover, while using the language of rights to argue for protection of women's right to bodily integrity, we suggest that in order to ensure justice an evenly applied notion of bodily integrity is in order. That is, bodily integrity should mean more than protection to be left alone in the private sphere; it should mean more than mere security. Bodily integrity should be a right grounded in security and possibility—the possibility of having access to health care, food, and shelter. We find that the term "domestic violence against women" may provide a symbolic and practical formulation of the problem of bodily harm by intimates that is useful in our current political climate. Only when bodily integrity can be secured within a context of the principled treatment of every "body" on an economic and social level will protection from bodily harm have substantial meaning for women. And only then will women's citizenship signal justice.

Chapter 3

Feminists Negotiate the Executive Branch: The Policing of Male Violence

Anne Sparks

> At least as important as deterring the abuser is the message [conveyed by mandatory arrest] to the woman who is beaten, to her children, to the neighbors and, indeed, to all of society, that no longer will woman abuse be ignored, no longer will society fail to treat it as the serious crime which it is. (Zorza and Woods 1994b, 9)

> Police action cannot by itself stem the tide of violence against women. It can, however, stop perpetuating and reproducing it. To do so would require breaking its links with other aspects of social life that maintain and perpetuate women's subordination. Police protection within the context of male domination does not and cannot promise women autonomy. (Stanko 1989, 67)

For two decades, feminists and battered women's advocates have conducted a vigilant, well-coordinated campaign to improve the police response to domestic violence. This chapter presents the history of these efforts, analyzes the strategies used, and discusses their impact. We examine policing as a social institution and point out connections between police culture, male dominance, and violence in the society at large. Throughout the chapter we trace the contradictions inherent in mobilizing the powers of law enforcement to bring about positive change for women.

As indicated by the quotations juxtaposed above, feminists do not agree on the importance or soundness of legally requiring police to arrest in domestic violence cases. (The commonly used term for such a requirement is "mandatory arrest.") The controversy about nation-wide implementation of mandatory arrest policies reflects the ambivalence with which feminists regard the police. On one hand, battered women's advocates want to hold the police accountable, as agents of the state, for carrying out the government's mandate to protect citizens. On the other hand, feminists realize that police often exercise their power in ways that reinforce the disadvantages already experienced by women, and in ways that reinforce the disadvantages experienced by members of poor and minority communities as well (Chambliss 1995; Florida Supreme Court, 1990). Given the predominance of men in the police force, feminists question whether police will truly cooperate in carrying out a policy designed to reduce the power that men exercise over women.

Reliance on the police to further the goal of empowering women has problematic and even paradoxical aspects; yet clearly the potential for improved police intervention on behalf of battered women cannot be ignored. Looking beyond concerns about the police to general criticisms of the criminal justice system made by battered women and their advocates, we realize that the system's emphasis on proving that a crime occurred and punishing the offender does not fit well with the needs of women experiencing domestic violence. Assurance that her "case" will eventually be tried in court is little comfort to a women whose former boyfriend is threatening to kill her. In their work to make the system more responsive to battered women, advocates are actually transforming its mandate. Redefining the purpose of the system according to the needs of battered women, they attempt to shift its primary orientation from that of carrying out an abstract standard of justice to one of providing protection and resources to those in danger. The difference between the focus on prosecution and the advocates' perspective can be characterized as the difference between "justice" and "care" orientations to ethical decisions identified by Carol Gilligan in her study of gender difference in moral development (Gilligan 1982).

Effective negotiation of the state requires analysis of its functions and relevant structures. Responsibilities of the state include defining and controlling criminal behavior. In examining the nature of the institutions that carry out these responsibilities, we find that they may act in discriminatory and oppressive ways. For example, although the police have a clear mandate to enforce the law, other aspects of their mandate, particularly that of "maintaining order" are open to interpretation. As a local agency with authority and with legitimate access to weapons and other means of coercion, the police force has the potential to function in a quasi-military role. Police can be summoned rapidly, in large numbers, in response to a protest, a crime, or any situation perceived to require police "back-up." As agents of social control, police have some degree of autonomy in how they exercise their power. They can abuse their power both by failing to act in some situations and by over-reacting in other situations.

The following sections lay the groundwork for evaluating the strategies feminists have developed to improve police intervention in domestic violence. First we analyze the police force as a political institution. Then we outline the major developments regarding police intervention and domestic violence over the past two decades and explore issues underlying the controversy about mandatory arrest. We ask three major questions: Is it likely that the police can bring about fundamental change in the social conditions that perpetuate violence against women? What consequences may result from giving the criminal justice system primary responsibility for reducing domestic violence? Where do feminists stand on the use of state power for social control?

Policing as a Site for Social Change

Police are the gate-keepers of the law enforcement and criminal justice systems. They implement (and interpret) the public mandate to maintain peace and order on the community level; they decide whether an incident becomes officially logged and processed as a crime; they determine who enters into criminal proceedings as the alleged criminal and who assumes the role of complainant (also called "victim-witness"). The impact of the police cannot be totally isolated from the impact of other components of the criminal justice system such as the prosecutor's office and defense attorneys, the courts (including judges who set bail, preside over trials, and sentence those convicted), and prison, probation, and parole. Therefore, general considerations regarding use of the criminal justice system in the interests of battered women and feminist goals, as well as the specific characteristics of the police force, are relevant to this discussion.

Since lawmakers represent the interests of dominant groups, the law reflects and maintains unequal power relations in society (Yeager 1995). If, overall, the legal system functions to perpetuate women's subordinate status within the nuclear family and the economy, attempts to create and enforce laws to help women escape from violent marriages will have limited success (Ferraro 1989). Without careful analysis, attempts to use the law and the criminal justice system to empower battered women may actually result in further victimization. We will discuss two important considerations in developing strategies regarding the police: ways in which the police force reflects and maintains patterns of dominance that exist in society, and ways in which police attitudes and procedures determine the police response to domestic violence.

Although women seek employment in police work at all levels, police departments remain male-dominated and, especially among the rank and file, steeped in "a 'macho-style' masculinity" (Stanko 1989, 52). Despite the increasing visibility of crimes against women and the number of women entering traditionally male occupations, "[P]olicing of men's violence against women...remains largely in the hands of men" (Stanko 1989, 46). The police force itself exemplifies the male dominance that underlies the problem of domestic violence.

Within institutions dominated by men, such as the military, college fraternities, and male athletics, aggression is often legitimized (and even glorified or ritualized). Since police often represent themselves as a fraternal order or brotherhood, aspects of fraternity culture are relevant to this analysis. College fraternities value qualities consistent with a narrow definition of masculinity such as competition, athleticism, dominance, and "militant heterosexuality"; they are preoccupied with loyalty, group protection, and secrecy (Martin and Hummer 1993, 118). Fraternity members forge bonds with one another "in physically and psychologically abusive rituals" (Sanday 1990, 172).

Clearly, in many contexts in our society, masculinity is linked with violence. Within fraternities, and within the police force, rigid definitions of masculine and feminine, devaluation of women, and emphasis on physical prowess contribute to an acceptance of some forms of male violence and male dominance over women. The question asked by a batterer in a mandated treatment program demonstrates the link between male socialization and violence against women: "Is the government that wants me to stop my violence the same one that trained me to kill in Vietman?" (Stark 1993, 658). One effect of male violence in our culture —the danger and harm experienced by women on a daily basis— cannot be significantly remedied without major transformations in the institutions that support male violence in general. Therefore, while better police intervention might help reduce domestic violence, the police force, as an institution, actually contributes to maintaining the problem.

Patterns of dominance and privilege in the society are both protected by and reproduced within police culture. As the criminal justice system is designed to protect and reinforce the existing social order, it cannot directly remedy problems within the social structure that perpetuate domestic violence. Those with greater wealth and social status often receive more favorable treatment, whether as victims or offenders. There is no standard that determines what help a victim should receive in seeking safety or how severely a suspect should be treated.

According to Ferraro (1993), the police have historically been agents in the oppression of people of color, poor people, and homosexuals. She notes that "violence is condemned most often when it violates existing power and institutional hierarchies" (Ferraro 1993, 165). If this is so, more aggressive policing of domestic violence cannot fail to have discriminatory effects. Since police generally deal more harshly with offenders from racial and ethnic minority groups and from lower income neighborhoods, pressure to increase arrests in domestic violence cases may exacerbate the use of police force in these communities, while middle class and white batterers may continue to be treated leniently (Ferraro 1993). Battered women may become even more vulnerable to severe penalties for inflicting injury or killing in self-defense. Furthermore, battering in gay and lesbian couples may continue to be ignored by the police (Ferraro 1993).

One source of difficulty in changing police practices is the hierarchical structure of police departments, particularly the gap between the administrative level which adopts policy and the rank and file level which implements it (Ferraro 1989; Stanko 1989). Another source of difficulty is the investment that police officers make in their arrests. The belief that arrests in "domestic cases" fail to result in successful prosecutions contributes to police reluctance to arrest in situations involving male violence against female partners (Ferraro 1989; Stanko 1989). Research conducted with on-duty rank and file officers in Phoenix, Arizona, found that the reasons given by individual officers for their reluctance to respond to calls for aid from battered women were similar to those cited in the literature on this issue. The reasons include danger, fear of being sued, low probability of prosecution, failure of wives to follow through on complaints, and "antipathy towards 'social work' versus crime fighting" (Ferraro 1989, 167).

Other traditional aspects of policing that limit the likelihood of effective responses to domestic violence are the use of gender-neutral definitions and the isolation of a specific incident to establish whether a crime was committed. In her study of police responses to calls of family fights, Ferraro (1993) found that the officers somewhat subjectively determine whether or not there is probable cause for arrest. After determining that probable cause exists (based on damaged property, evidence that a weapon was used, or evidence of injury, for example), they then decide who is at fault. "If they view each partner as equally liable, both parties will be arrested. The neutrality of legal language provides the context for police to view women battering as 'mutual combat' and the arrest of women as appropriate" (Ferraro 1993, 169). The practice of arresting both parties involved in the domestic violence is termed "dual arrest."

Police intervention requires designation of a specific unit of time as the "domestic violence incident." This "incident" is abstracted from the life history of a couple. Therefore, the man's tactics of intimidation and control in the relationship and any pattern of escalating violence (which could be the basis for a woman's acts of self defense) are not considered relevant (Sheptychi 1993).

Feminist Efforts to Change the Police Response

To understand the obstacles initially faced by activists who sought to improve the police response to domestic violence, we begin with the historic relegation of intra-family violence to non-criminal proceedings (Edwards 1989). The separation of the system established to address abuse and other problems within families from the system dealing with "real crimes" effectively prevented battered women from getting police help in the early 1970s (when feminists began organizing speak-outs on rape, incest, and domestic violence.) Although the reality of widespread violence against women began to seep into public consciousness, police continued to give low priority to "domestic calls." When they did respond, officers frequently attempted to mediate between the partners, or else separated them briefly (by ordering the male to leave the premises). In the few cases that came to court, the judge often ordered the couple to undergo mediation (counseling focused on "resolving differences"). A woman who did receive an order of protection or restraining order (ordering the assailant to stay away from her) often had to serve the order (that is, physically present it to the assailant) herself. The orders were usually not enforced by the police.

Zorza (1992) details the formal and informal policies in police departments throughout the United States that well into the 1970s discouraged police from responding to "domestic calls." One aspect of violence against partners, marital rape, was not even considered against the law anywhere in the country until 1981 when the supreme courts of Massachusetts and New Jersey ruled that a husband could be criminally liable for raping his wife (Zorza 1992). Even with the advent of formal police training and social pressure to respond to domestic violence as a crime, educating the police has been difficult. Many police officers not only dismiss woman battering as a real crime, they are guilty of it themselves "or tolerate it within their ranks" (Zorza 1992, 52). Battered women's advocates know that a policeman's battered wife is especially vulnerable, "since most other officers will fail to protect her or enforce any protective order that she may have obtained" (Zorza 1992, 52).

Three lawsuits have been credited with convincing police departments all over the country to revise their policies and improve their response to battered women. In 1976, a class action suit was filed by the Legal Aid Society against the Chief of the Oakland (California) Police Department on behalf of "women in general and black women in particular who are victims of domestic violence" (Zorza 1992, 54). All five named plaintiffs were black women who had received no response, an ineffectual response, or a threatening response from police to their calls for protection when beaten up by a husband, ex-husband, or boyfriend. (The lawyers were able to allege a denial of the equal protection mandated by the Fourteenth Amendment by arguing that the police response to black victims was less adequate than the response to white victims.) Three years after the suit was filed, the parties agreed to a settlement which created new police policy. This included responding quickly to domestic violence calls, making an arrest when an officer had probable cause to believe that a felonious assault had occurred or that a misdemeanor had been committed in his presence, informing battered women of their right to make a citizen's arrest and of community services for victims, and enforcing civil restraining orders (Zorza 1992, 56). The suit served a dual strategic purpose, "to obtain effective police protection for battered women...and to educate not only the criminal justice system, but also the public, about the problem of domestic violence" (Gee 1983, 554).

A similar suit in New York City, also filed in 1976, targeted the Family Court and the Probation Department as well as the Police Department which entered into a consent judgment with the plaintiffs. The judgment provided for adequate police response to requests by women for protection from violent acts by their husbands. It states, "When the officer has reasonable cause to believe that a husband committed a felony against his wife or violated an order of protection, the officer must arrest him and should not attempt to reconcile the parties or mediate" (Zorza 1992, 59). As a result of these two successful lawsuits, police departments throughout the United States began listening to demands from battered women's advocates and lawyers for effective police intervention in domestic violence cases, in order to avoid being sued.

Those police departments that had not responded to the message delivered by the Oakland and New York City suits were forced by the settlement in *Thurman v. City of Torrington, Connecticut*[1] to face the possibility of huge liability unless they changed their policies. In this widely publicized case, Tracey Thurman was awarded $2.3 million by a federal jury "because the police were negligent in failing to protect her from her abusive husband" (Zorza 1992, 60). Thurman had moved to Connecticut to escape her violent marriage. Her husband followed her there and became well known to the police as a result of attacks and threats against his estranged wife who appropriately obtained a restraining order against him. She suffered permanent scarring and paralysis as the result of his most violent assault, prior to which she made an emergency call to the police. The court found that the town and the police had maintained a "policy of indifference" that amounted to sex discrimination (Zorza 1992, 60).

In the wake of these landmark decisions, battered women's advocates worked on the community level to help police departments develop effective domestic violence policies and on the state level to enact laws enabling police to arrest when responding to domestic incidents (Zorza 1992). While most legislation was being framed to allow officers to arrest in misdemeanor cases when the offense was not committed in the officer's presence and when the officer had probable cause to believe that a protection order had been violated, the Oregon Coalition Against Domestic and Sexual Violence took a different approach. It proposed a bill *requiring* police officers to arrest "anyone in a domestic violence incident whom the officer had probable cause to believe had committed an assault or had placed a victim with an order of protection in fear of imminent serious physical injury" (Zorza 1992, 63). Passage of the bill in 1977 made Oregon the first state to require police arrest in domestic violence cases. This is the beginning of what is known as "mandatory arrest."

In 1980 Oregon activists filed suit because the police were not conforming to the law. The Oregon Supreme Court held that police did not have discretion in enforcing restraining orders. As a result, every police department in Oregon was required to adopt a mandatory arrest policy, and similar developments occurred in other states (Zorza 1992). Increased public awareness of the plight of battered women spurred efforts to develop preventive measures. Public as well as private funds became available for developing programs and conducting research. Groups in Duluth, Minnesota, established a coordinated community response to domestic violence that included mandatory arrest and treatment for the batterer. Although this approach improved rates of prosecution and deterred repeat offenses (Pence and Shepard 1988), it was overlooked by the National Institute of Justice (NIJ) which chose instead to fund six replications of an experiment in Minneapolis. That study had shown that arrest alone had a significant deterrent effect on batterers[2] (Sherman and Berk 1984).

Expert opinions on the results of the completed replication studies vary. Some analysts believe the results support the original study's findings, and others claim that the results of the replications are inconclusive or actually show that arrest can increase the likelihood of violence in certain communities (Buzawa and Buzawa 1993b). The National Battered Women's Law Project of the National Center on Women and Family Law reports that the NIJ studies show that arrest is generally superior to other interventions by the police as a method of deterring future violence (Zorza and Woods 1994a, 1). Some feminists have criticized the studies for not including input from battered women's advocates, and for attempting to study the effects of arrest in isolation rather than in conjunction with services to victims and aggressive prosecution (Bowman 1992; Lerman 1992; Zorza 1992; Hart 1993). Besides the study of Duluth mentioned above, feminists favorably cite research in London, Ontario, which found that a comprehensive approach reduced recidivism among batterers (Jaffe, Hastins, Reitzel, and Austin 1993; Zorza and Woods 1994b).

How have battered women themselves responded to the new arrest policy in domestic violence cases? Previously, a victim of domestic violence had suddenly found herself in a strange, seemingly powerful position, *if* the seriousness of the incident warranted arrest, and she agreed to press charges. In other words, it was up to the battered women, if the police saw cause to arrest, whether or not the batterer *was* actually arrested (unless a felony had been committed, or the police had witnessed the assault.) Once the arrest was made, the assailant (and his family and sometimes his attorney) tried to talk or scare the battered woman out of proceding with the complaint. At the same time, police and prosecutors often tried to convince her that it was her duty to follow through as the complaining witness—otherwise the case would have to be dropped. Meanwhile, the woman had no assurance regarding how long the batterer would be kept in jail (frequently he would be freed without her being notified). If he were not in jail, she often had no way to protect herself from retaliation for the arrest; if she wanted to enter a shelter for battered women she probably learned that space is not always available, and length of stay is limited. The battered woman, if dependent on income from the man for rent, mortgage payments, and/or child support, often faced a financial crisis, which would be used by the batterer as leverage to get her to drop charges. If the batterer were the father of the woman's children, whether or not the couple lived together, she could also be made to feel guilty for "doing this to the children's father."[3]

Under mandatory arrest or pro-arrest policy, the police do not ask the woman if she is willing to press charges, but arrest on the basis of determining probable cause and fault, as discussed earlier. Of course, the woman's cooperation and possible testimony in court will probably be necessary in order to convict the batterer, but the initial responsibility for "treating the batterer like a criminal" is taken by the police. There are varying accounts of how this change has affected battered women. Mandatory arrest or pro-arrest policies can disempower women "despite the best intentions of their advocates," according to Sheptychi (1993, 132). Dual arrests, in which both parties in the "domestic disturbance" are arrested, are an example of the way mandatory arrest policies may backfire.

Unfortunately, pro-arrest policies do not always reflect commitment to the notions that the community, not the battered woman, should take responsibility for the arrest of the batterer, and that police should be accountable to battered women. The program in Duluth, Minnesota, considered by some to be an ideal model, succeeded because feminists worked in conjunction with battered women to develop and gain community support for it (Pence and Shepard 1988). Merely adopting a pro-arrest policy alone may signal a primary focus on law enforcement, rather than community involvement and empowerment of battered women, as the "solution" to domestic violence (Ferraro and Pope 1993; Sheptychi 1993).

The impact of mandatory arrest on the battered woman is just as important as its impact on the batterer, according to feminists. Zorza has criticized NIJ's replication studies (in Milwaukee, Omaha, and Charlotte) for failing to take into account "how the female victims' responses to the various police actions may have affected the overall results" (Zorza 1992, 67). The theory behind this criticism is that women who find the criminal justice system responsive to their wishes will continue to call upon it as needed, which presumably will lessen their vulnerability to serious injury. Research reported by Gondolf and Fisher on the effectiveness of batterer treatment programs found that "fifty-three percent of women plan to reconcile with a batterer-in-treatment, but only nineteen percent of abused women plan to do so if the batterer is not in treatment" (cited in Zorza 1992, 67). While this research found that treatment does *not* deter battering, and victims, of course, might reconcile with their "treated" batterers believing that it does, Zorza argues that the important finding was that "women whose partners were sent to court-ordered treatment were more likely to call police and bring new charges if they were subsequently assaulted" (Zorza 1992, 67). According to her reasoning, mandating the treatment is important, therefore, not to change the batterer, but because the victim is more likely to call the police for help in the future "knowing that the criminal justice system acted once in the past to support her" (Zorza 1992, 67).[4] This is an excellent example of how feminist advocates evaluate the functioning of the criminal justice system from the victim's (that is, the battered woman's) perspective, rather than in terms of its abstract social purpose or its impact on the criminal alone.

Before addressing the issues involved in evaluating what feminists have accomplished by demanding more aggressive policing of domestic violence against women, it is important to note the extensive adoption of mandatory arrest laws and policies and their impact. Fourteen states and the District of Columbia now have laws mandating police arrest under specific conditions in domestic violence incidents. Twenty states require police to arrest when the defendant has violated an order of protection (Zorza and Woods 1994b). In general, both numbers of arrests and demands for services from programs helping battered women have increased dramatically in states that mandate arrest. For instance, in Iowa, three years following institution of mandatory arrest, police were making almost three times as many referrals to shelters as they had previously made. Rates of prosecution have increased, placing more demands on the courts, and drawing attention to their functioning. At the same time, feminists have deplored an increase in dual arrests and arrests of women in some states. For instance, in Kansas City, the arrest rate for women in domestic violence incidents rose from 10% to 20% following the implementation of a mandatory arrest policy[5] (Zorza and Woods 1994b, 18). The fact that women have been wrongfully arrested heightens concerns about batterers' successful lawsuits for child custody[6] (Zorza and Woods 1994b; New Jersey Coalition for Battered Women 1994).

Feminism and Use of State Power for Social Control

The feminist campaign for an aggressive police response to domestic violence has puzzled some analysts who find it contradictory (Edwards 1989; Buzawa and Buzawa 1993a). The current feminist effort to end male violence against female partners has its roots in the women's liberation movement. Many women who devoted themselves to raising consciousness and ending sexism in the late 1960s and early 1970s worked for other "pro-liberation" causes as well. They actively opposed government intervention in women's lives, advocating reproductive choice, decriminalization of homosexuality, and legalization of prostitution. Many women's liberation activists had opposed the war in Vietnam and continued to campaign against military intervention by the United States in other countries. (For example, while opposed by the U.S. government, the socialist revolution in Nicaragua received widespread support from many activist groups, including feminist organizations, who perceived it as an anti-colonial struggle). In these causes, feminism has aligned with groups typically characterized as the left wing of the political spectrum, which generally opposes the use of state power for social control. The belief that society needs "tough laws" and an aggressive police force to maintain social order is associated with the right wing of the political spectrum. Edwards (1989) notes that the goals of decreasing crime and establishing rights for crime victims are related in some ways to the "law and order" agenda of the political right.[7] In the debate over mandatory arrest, feminists are challenged to reconcile increasing police power to enforce laws against domestic violence with recognition that this power can be exercised in oppressive ways, particularly in communities whose members lack political power.

Results from the NIJ replication studies in Omaha, Milwaukee, and Charlotte indicate that arrest may significantly increase subsequent violence in some offenders (Buzawa and Buzawa 1993a). Sherman, one of the researchers from the original Minneapolis Study, reversed his pro-mandatory arrest position for this reason. He concludes from the results of the studies that arrest is more likely to have a crime reduction effect on employed suspects than on unemployed suspects. The findings suggest that men with jobs do not want to jeopardize their employment by behaving in a way that is likely to get them arrested. He argues that among those suspects whose connections to society are already weak, it is more likely that arrest will backfire by causing increased violence (Buzawa and Buzawa 1993a; Schmidt and Sherman 1993). Based on the Milwaukee replication study, Sherman cautions that mandatory arrest policies "may disproportionally place inner-city black women in increased danger" (cited in Buzawa and Buzawa 1993b, 345).

The most problematic issue in advocating for increased police power to arrest is how such power is likely to be exercised in minority communities and high poverty areas where incidents involving racism, indifference, and brutality on the part of the police are all too frequent. Various discussions in the literature are relevant to the potential impact of more aggressive policing on such communities and the need for feminist strategy to address the race and class bias prevalent throughout the criminal justice system. Presently, however, these discussions do not constitute a unified feminist approach to this issue, or even a fully developed critique. The major themes in these discussions will be outlined below, followed by an examination of the goals of the mandatory arrest policy and reflections on what feminists have accomplished through their engagement with the criminal justice system.

As Chapter One describes, grass-roots activists in the shelter movement worked outside traditional institutions to establish "alternative" types of organizations and programs (Reinelt 1995). Many leaders of the original movement shared a vision of society that involved changing the economic system and eliminating all forms of oppression, not only sexism. Advocating for women whose lives were in danger brought these feminist groups into direct contact with the police and courts, and as funding for programs serving victims of crime became available, advocates working within the legal system on behalf of battered women also joined the movement. (Among all the groups now addressing violence against women, there still exists a tension between those committed to maintaining alternative programs and those working within traditional, bureaucratic institutions, although in actuality, many activists have done both).

Early leaders of the shelter and anti-rape movements generally rejected reliance on the criminal justice system to end violence against women. They believed that such a solution would require creation of "a totally repressive society" (Friedman 1979, 16). It would also involve unacceptable pressure on all victims to report their cases to the police, it would not address the conditions underlying violence against women, and it would not change other patterns of domination in society. Reliance on the criminal justice system should not be promoted, according to Friedman, because the system's purpose "has little to do with the protection of women or citizens"; under our legal system, "when a crime is committed, the injury is to the state" (Friedman 1979, 17).

A statement of principles by the organizers of the 1978 "March to Stop Violence Against Women" encourages communities to demand more foot patrols, bilingual and bicultural police, and officials (including women) who are sensitive to women's specific needs. At the same time, the organizers argue that, "Until those agencies are accountable to women and to the community at large—until they respond to priorities set by the people and not by themselves—we must not rely on the criminal justice system to stop violence against women" (D.C. Area Feminist Alliance Task Force on Violence Against Women 1979, 39). The major strategies endorsed in the statement are increasing women's economic self-sufficiency, learning and teaching self-defense, and developing "ways to insititutionalize community censure of violence against women" (D.C. Area Feminist Alliance Task Force on Violence Against Women 1979, 41).

Early movement leaders distinguished between reforms that contribute to lasting fundamental change, and reforms that, taken as goals in themselves, merely perpetuate oppressive structures. For example, the goal of increasing arrest and conviction rates for rapists and batterers without simultaneously making the criminal justice system more accountable to people of color and poor people, or without organizing and educating in order to empower women through their involvement with the system, would be considered "reformist" only. That is, the goal in itself would not constitute a step towards a more just distribution of power in the society overall (Friedman 1979; Bunch 1979). According to the criteria developed by these activists, feminists should choose specific strategies according to their potential to empower women. Empowerment, however, means different things to different women. This becomes clear upon examining the meaning of police involvement to women from various communities.

Women who distrust the police are not likely to call them for help. If the police are called by someone else, cooperation may well depend upon the demeanor of the police and perhaps the presence of a female officer.[8] In communities where the police are generally regarded with mistrust, few people will benefit from public education regarding the fact that domestic violence is a crime. Stanko (1989) urges feminists to pressure police to improve their relationship with poor and minority communities so that more battered women will make use of the police.

Minority groups that experience discrimination and whose traditions and cultural integrity are not respected by the larger society may discourage their members from using the criminal justice system to deal with the wrongdoings of others in the community (Rios 1995). Battered women themselves may prefer not to subject their batterers to the criminal justice system, knowing that the system may act with excessive harshness in dealing with men from that community. Feminists advocate that these women should not be pressured to cooperate with prosecution (Hart 1993). Some women may find the isolation of their ethnic or religious group oppressive, especially if women's roles in the culture are very limited. This does not mean, however, that they want to, or can, sever ties with their community. In providing outreach and services to battered women in such situations, it is important for feminists to be aware of cultural norms and to respect women's cultural identifications and ties with their community (Martinez 1979; Rios 1995).

Although much of the controversy about mandatory arrest centers on the impact of the police in minority and poor communities, voices of battered women and activists in these communities have not been prominent in this debate. To what extent do minority and low income groups actually participate in the ongoing movement against domestic violence? Activists from minority communities have had some success in establishing community-based programs (Violence Intervention Program 1995). They have also helped more mainstream programs to develop services that are responsive to the needs of diverse populations. For example, a Native American social worker describes her work teaching "Anglos" tribally appropriate ways of running groups on battering and sexual abuse:

> [O]ne way of dealing with a batterer is to have one of the wife's relatives move in with her and to send the husband to live with his relatives. Every time a non-Indian feminist tells us, without understanding Indian family values or how our system can be used, to "break away" from batterers, they are saying our values and our culture are unimportant. (Sears 1992, 8)

Buzawa and Buzawa (1993a) believe that mandatory arrest policies inherently reinforce an existing class bias in overall arest rates. They find it ironic that academics and feminists, known for their liberal views and distrust of the police as an institution, now endorse changes that increase involvement of the police in "intimate disputes and family violence . . . despite some evidence that police (have) often used such statutes more often against minority and disadvantaged males rather than against other offenders" (Buzawa and Buzawa 1993a, 568). Some feminists have expressed concern that mandating arrest may result in men of color being arrested at disproportionately higher rates than white men. Although Zorza and Woods (1994b) cite studies showing that this has not occurred, they do not discuss potentially discriminatory treatment after arrest, such as conformity with due process, availability of qualified public defenders, setting of bail, access to rehabilitation, and severity of sentencing (Clear 1996).

Feminist Support for Mandatory Arrest

In response to the concerns raised by Sherman, some feminists have stated that they never considered arrest alone sufficient to deter future violence, but as a step that has to be followed up with prosecution and sentencing. Advocates recognize the need to increase services to battered women so that those women who are most at risk following arrest can make adequate plans for their own and their children's safety. Exemplary legislation in Connecticut provides a Family Violence Victim Advocate program in the courts "focused on empowerment and assisting women [to] develop and implement safety plans" (Zorza and Woods 1994b, 27). Many feminists believe that mandatory arrest is a meaningful signal not only to batterers but to the whole society that domestic violence is a crime, and that laws against assault will be enforced both inside and outside the home (Zorza and Woods 1994b, 9).

Stark asks what the battered women's movement hoped to accomplish through bringing about change in police procedure:

> After all, having established an unprecedented woman-run, community-based alternative service movement, why risk losing our identity by placing so much emphasis on a male-run system ...located on the far right of the political spectrum in terms of community participation, access to influence, attitudes toward women, and bureaucratic isolation? (Stark 1993, 660-661)

In answer to his own question, Stark states that arrest provides "a meaningful opportunity for battered women to consider their options" and time to go elsewhere or to obtain a protective order (Stark 1993, 662). He states that the policy of mandatory arrest sets "a standard of zero tolerance for battering" and notes that under deterrence theory, its function "is to convey the criminal nature of battering" (Stark 1993, 662). Stark believes that mandatory arrest also redistributes the services of the police, making them available to women "on a more egalitarian basis" (Stark 1993, 663).

Stark's response to critics concerned about the potential danger of extending the state's social control is that noninterference itself is a form of control:

> Whether criminal justice intervention will be defined as "control" or "liberation" depends on the reference group. From the standpoint of women whose personal lives are governed by norms of male dominance supported by structural inequities, noninterference functions to exacerbate control. Conversely, outside intervention that challenges existing power relations is a fundamental precondition for autonomy among the oppressed. (Stark 1993, 677)

The idea that the police force can be used as outside intervention against male violence in the "private domain" reminds us of the paradox involved in using state power. Is Stark saying that men in the police force will "liberate" women from their abusive male partners, even though some of these same policemen may also be batterers at home?

Reframing mandatory arrest as a way of redistributing criminal justice resources is an interesting alternative to the discourse of social control. However, it is not a totally satisfactory response to specific, documented concerns about how police exercise their power. More important than this "redistribution" is the fact that in claiming access to criminal justice resources for women, feminists also bring into question the functions of the institutions themselves, and the constructions of justice and protection upon which they are based. For example, Hart explains that battered women, knowing that the batterer's arrest alone is no guarantee of their safety,

> may thus be much more concerned about preventing future violence than about vindicating the state's interest in penalizing the defendant for crimes previously committed. This orientation of the battered woman toward future safety may create a tension with those in the criminal justice system singularly focused on winning criminal convictions. (Hart 1993, 626)

Evaluating Feminist Efforts to Improve the Policing of Domestic Violence

Mandatory arrest policies have not totally changed the basis of police decision-making, and thus they do not signal a redefinition of crime intervention that takes into consideration structural inequalities in society. However, the criminalization of domestic violence is a crucial accomplishment from which debates about mandatory arrest should not detract. Feminists deserve credit for the fact that attacks by men on their current or former wives or girlfriends are no longer called "domestic disputes" by the police. When they receive such a report, police are now prepared to arrest one person for assaulting another rather than mediate. In addition to progress establishing that criminal sanctions apply to male violence against female partners, feminist negotiation of the criminal justice system implicitly questions and transforms the system's mandate. When battered women's advocates call for use of arrest as a way of guaranteeing a battered woman time to get to a safe place, and when they say that she needs supportive services in order to follow through on prosecution, or needs the discretion to withdraw from prosecuting, according to her view of her own best interest, *these* are radical and humanizing expectations which imply that the system can be made accountable to citizens, rather than to abstract principles of justice.

Before ending on a visionary note, however, we must pay serious attention to the amount of effort (for example, in organizing, fund raising, lobbying, counseling, advocating, training, and monitoring) that this approach to social change has taken and will continue to take, if any accomplishments are to last. In advising feminists to be "flexible and wary" in utilizing existing structures such as the criminal justice system, Ferraro states,

> A focus on increased policing of battering has the potential to divert attention from the sources of violence [in the society] to its individual perpetrators...[E]nhanced police protection...will not change the structural conditions that perpetuate male violence and women's economic dependence on violent males. (Ferraro 198, 180-182)

How many prisons are we willing to build for batterers? Feminist efforts to date have not succeeded in decreasing the overall incidence of domestic violence against women, and current efforts are threatened by a backlash phenomenon. We need to think carefully about, and possibly separate, specific strategies to protect women in imminent danger, to empower women in general, and to end male violence against women.

The next chapter discusses feminist engagement with the judicial branch of government, focusing on treatment by the courts of women who have killed their batterers. Just as the police, responding to a call, designate one segment of time as the crime incident, the courts traditionally focused on the action of the woman defendant only at one moment—that is, when she killed—rather than considering how she had been affected by previous violence or the ongoing context of danger within which she acted. As a result of feminist efforts, the courts began to allow testimony regarding previous incidents and the effects of repeated violence on battered women.

Chapter 4

Feminists Negotiate the Judicial Branch: Battered Woman's Syndrome

Paris De Soto

> Ironically, the most complete description of women's suffering from domestic violence has entered our case law and legal literature at the point where violence against women finally harms men—when battered women kill in self-defense. (Mahoney 1991, 35)

The battered woman who kills her batterer is a complex and controversial defendant, usually portrayed as part vigilante, part victim, part madwoman. She is Francine Hughes, who poured kerosene around the bed of her sleeping husband and lit the bed on fire; this act was done on the same night Mrs. Hughes was smeared with food and garbage and raped by Mr. Hughes. She is Leslie Emick, who shot her sleeping husband; three days before the shooting, Mrs. Emick was burned with an electric immersion coil in her vagina, nearly hanged in a shed, and struck in the head with a mallet by Mr. Emick (Ewing 1987, 3–10). For these and many other battered women, it seems as though "til death do us part" is their only way out of these domestic nightmares.

What happens when these women present their cases to the courts? Francine Hughes pleaded not guilty by reason of temporary insanity and was acquitted from the charge of first degree murder. Leslie Emick argued that she acted out of self-defense and was charged with first degree manslaughter. Although the testimony of a physician and a psychiatrist presented the jury with clear evidence of Emick's physical and psychological torture, and the psychiatrist carefully outlined the battered woman's syndrome from which Emick suffered, the prosecution won, maintaining that "the very ongoing nature of the abuse prove[d] that Miss Emick was under no imminent danger, particularly from a sleeping man" (Ewing 1987, 3). On appeal and as part of a plea bargain, Emick's sentence was reduced from several years in prison to five years of probation. Emick's case is not unusual. Studies show that 72 to 80 percent of battered women who kill their abusers are convicted or accept a plea, and many receive long, harsh sentences (Osthoff 1992, 2).

Clearly, justice has not been served in cases such as Emick's. Because the law currently defines such terms as "imminent danger" and "self-defense" from a man's perspective, battered women defendants are at a significant disadvantage. As Susan Edwards points out, society punishes stringently those women who violate cultural demands for conformity and whose private lives "depart from conventional profiles of domesticity, motherhood, and wifehood" (1989, 13). To counteract the sex-bias in the legal system, psychologists and legal scholars have worked resolutely to initiate the concept of battered woman's syndrome into the courts.

The Clinical Definition of Battered Woman's Syndrome

Battered woman's syndrome (BWS) is a psychological phenomenon that was first introduced to the courts in 1979 (Schuller and Vidmar 1992, 273). More specifically, BWS is a "descriptive term that refers to a pattern of responses and perceptions presumed to be characteristic of women who have been subjected to continuous physical abuse by their mate" (Schuller and Vidmare 1992, 274). BWS has been increasingly used—where and when it is admissible—as part of the defense of a battered woman who kills her abusive partner. Although some legal scholars find dubious the existence of such a syndrome (see Morse 1990; Faigman 1986), enough clinical evidence exists to make BWS an admissible part of the woman's defense in most states (Walker 1993, 253). BWS has been recognized as a subtype of Post-Traumatic Stress Disorder since 1980 in the American Psychiatric Association's *Diagnostic and Statistical Manual* (Dutton and Goodman 1994, 216). Leonore Walker, a clinical psychologist who has been an expert witness of BWS in nearly 300 trials in the United States, has thoroughly established a symptomology of the syndrome, including a cycle of battering. She articulates the complex psychological reasons in addition to economic, social, and legal factors which make leaving the abusive relationship difficult for the battered woman, if not impossible.

In her research, Walker has borrowed the term "learned helplessness" (Seligman 1975) to describe the "process of victimization [that] is perpetuated to the point of psychological paralysis" (Walker 1979, 43). In many situations, because the battered woman perceives that she has no control over her batterer's abusive behavior, she begins to grow almost numb and gives in to the abuse. She may try to escape at first, which tends to lead only to more abuse, but eventually she becomes compliant and passive. As Walker describes, the battered woman thinks, "'No matter what I do, I have no influence.' She cannot think of alternatives. She says, 'I am incapable and too stupid to learn how to change things'" (Walker 1979, 50). Walker observes that some battered women, although they accept their beatings as inevitable, try to control the time and place of the beatings and thus garner a small sense of feeling other than total helplessness. For example, the woman will do something she knows will provoke her partner (such as nagging or not cooking dinner) so that she may be somewhat more prepared for his attacks on her.

The Three Phases of the Battering Cycle

Walker has separated the battering cycle of the abusive relationship into three separate phases: the tension-building phase; the explosion or acute battering incident; and the calm, loving respite (Walker 1979, 55). The first phase, the tension-building phase, tends to last longest. Minor battering incidents occur, after which the woman will either act more compliant or try to get out of her batterer's way. If she can accommodate his demands effectively enough, she may prevent him from angrier, more aggressive actions. If she doesn't accommodate his demands adequately, when he does explode, she assumes the guilt. As Walker notes,

> She has become his accomplice by accepting some of the responsibility for his abusive behavior. She is not interested in the reality of the situation, because she is desperately attempting to prevent him from hurting her more. In order for her to sustain this role, she must not permit herself to get angry with the batterer. She resorts to a very common psychological defense—called, of course, "denial" by psychologists. (1979, 56)

From the batterer's perspective, according to Walker, once he sees her "apparent passive acceptance of this abusive behavior" he does nothing to change his behavior or to control his anger. Thus the tension between the batterer and his female partner only escalates during phase one until the batterer explodes. In phase one, the batterer can justify his minor beatings as a way of keeping the woman in line. However, his rage in phase two is so extreme that it blinds his control over his behavior and he severely beats her (Walker 1979, 60). After the acute battering incident, the batterer will try to blame his behavior on the petty annoyances the woman caused him during phase one, or he will blame drinking or overwork. This second phase of the battering cycle is much shorter than the first or third phase, lasting from two to twenty-four hours, and is much more violent. It is immediately followed by phase three, the phase of calm and the batterer's contrition.

During phase three, the batterer accepts responsibility for his extremely abusive actions. If his female partner is in the hospital, he will typically send her several bouquets of flowers and visit her often. If she is unresponsive, he will try to work on her guilt, telling her that she is his only hope and that without her he will be destroyed. It is during this time that the battered woman will most often escape because she knows that if he does find her, he may still be apologetic and suppliant—rather than enraged, menacing, and destructive. Yet this is also the phase that may convince her to stay. During phase three she gets a "glimpse of her original dream of how wonderful love is" (Walker 1979, 67). The batterer's loving, charming, and penitent behavior is her reinforcement for staying in the relationship. Furthermore, the battered woman may have almost no self-esteem and frustratingly limited access to financial support. During this phase, her batterer works on these areas, showering her with love and compliments and promising to take good care of her.

Inevitably, phase three ends and phase one begins again. The majority of battered women who kill their batterers kill them during this relapse in the batterer's abusive behavior. According to Walker, only a very small percentage of battered women reach the point in which they believe that "killing is the only way for them to stay alive." Walker emphasizes: "The goal of the battered woman who kills is to stop the abuse, not to kill the man" (1993, 234, 238).

It should be noted that Walker's cycle model is not applicable to all cases of domestic violence against women. For example, Walker's model does not fit cases where the man antagonizes and abuses the woman after she has ended the relationship. In place of Walker's model, some activist organizations, such as the Domestic Abuse Intervention Project in Duluth,

Minnesota, use a pie-chart model, in which each section identifies a specific battering behavior: emotional abuse, economic abuse, sexual abuse, using children, threats, using male privilege, intimidation, and isolation. By labelling the radius of this pie POWER AND CONTROL and the circumference PHYSICAL ABUSE, this model serves to illustrate more clearly the inner and outer cores of domestic violence.[1] With the pie-chart model, a battered woman can more easily recognize (and thereby work to resolve) her specific situation, rather than trying to force her experience to fit a three-phase cycle.

The Separation of the Public and the Private Sphere

According to the findings of the Maryland Special Joint Committee on Gender Bias in the Courts, "Victims of domestic violence often face a judicial system which does not believe that what they have suffered is a crime. They are treated differently from assault victims who were attacked by a stranger" (1989, 4). As we have discussed throughout this project, the binary opposition between the public and the private conceals the patriarchal base of the state. With an issue such as domestic violence against women, we can see how the private realm is posited as ideologically separate from the public realm—less so with the police, courts, and legislature now because of feminist insistence that "the personal is political," but certainly still with the batterers themselves. As Walker points out, the batterer is aware of his inappropriate behavior, "even if he does not acknowledge it." Walker continues: "Most batterers are only violent *in their own homes*. They understand all too well that *such behavior would not be tolerated in public*" (1979, 57, emphasis added). It should be noted that during the period of Walker's initial research in the 1970s, an arrest of the batterer was not mandatory, and restraining orders against the batterer were not effectively enforced, if they were even granted at all. The police and the courts were reluctant to get involved with "private" matters between domestic partners. Osthoff points out the double bind of domestic violence victims who kill their batterers: "When battered women kill their abusers, the same criminal justice system that often could not protect them vigorously prosecutes them as violent criminals" (1992, 3).

The police's reluctance to interfere in cases of domestic violence against women is only exacerbated for women who are neither white nor straight nor middle-class. As observed in the previous chapter, women in poor and marginalized communities often do not trust the police because they recognize the multiple biases against them—based not only on gender, but on race, class, and sexual preference. Thus these women tend to be reluctant to involve the police in their abusive domestic situations. For instance, in her discussion of lesbian battering, Martha Mahoney observes: "Homophobia in society deters many battered lesbians from invoking the legal system by calling the police for help or attempting to arrest the batterer" (Mahoney 1991, 50; see also Ferraro 1993, 168; Renzetti 1993). Evelyn Barbee notes that black women are less likely to use law enforcement, shelters, or human service personnel than they are to use medical facilities (1992, 161). Barbee emphasizes that African-American women are socialized not to share their concerns or problems outside the family/friend network (162). Moreover, African-American women may feel pressured not to "expose internal conflict that might reflect negatively on the black community" (Crenshaw, 1992: 420). Since this code of silence is a "self-imposed gesture of racial solidarity," a battered black woman who reports a case of domestic violence is "illustrated...as a traitor for coming forward with her story" (420).

When battered black women must be involved with the law not as victims, but as defendants, the courts' prejudices negatively influence the women's cases. Kimberle Crenshaw points out two significant disadvantages African-American women face in the courts. Because black women are stereotypically more "promiscuous" than white women, and because the U.S. legal system has drawn, historically, a connection between lack of chastity and lack of veracity, it is likely that an African-Amerian woman's testimony in court will not be believed (1992, 412–413). Battered black women who kill their partners are twice as likely to be convicted of murder and are given longer prison sentences than battered women who are white or of other minority groups (Walker 1993, 250; see also Bourg and Stock 1994).

Insanity Plea or Self-Defense?

As mentioned earlier, BWS has been offered to the courts as a mental disorder excusing criminal responsibility by virtue of an insanity defense. As an insanity defense, BWS has met with only limited success, but from a feminist perspective, it is a failure politically, socially, and philosophically. For one thing, the use of testimony on BWS as a mental disorder may reinforce negative myths about the sickness or frailty of women (Schneider 1980, 638). As Mary Ann Dutton and Lisa Goodman note: "When a battered woman's reaction to violence is framed as a 'syndrome' or 'disorder,' the unintended result may be...an image of pathology or diminished capacity when it may be not only inaccurate, but indeed the opposite of what is intended" (Dutton and Goodman 1994, 229). Most if not all feminist scholars insist that BWS should be used as an argument for justification of homicide rather than as an excuse for homicide (see Mahoney 1991; Littleton 1989). The difference between justification and excuse is crucial when approaching the battered woman as defendant. Schneider explains:

> Justified behavior is correct and appropriate, not only tolerated by the law but encouraged...by contrast, an excusable act is one that, although wrong, should be tolerated because of the actor's characteristics. The actor claiming excuse says, "I didn't mean to do it" or "I couldn't help myself"; the focus of excuse is on the actor's inability to avoid committing the offense. (1980, 630–631)

The excuse defense has had harmful repercussions for the battered woman who kills because "acquittal on these grounds often leads to involuntary commitment to mental health institutions" (Schneider 1980, 638). Furthermore, feminist legal activists rightly acknowledge that the excuse defense is demeaning in its implications that the battered woman who kills is insane, when she is justly taking action to save her own life (Walker 1993, 241).

Sex Bias in Legal Definitions

In cases where BWS is the defense, the difference between justification and excuse is the difference between self-defense and an insanity plea. Feminist legal advocates argue that feelings, perceptions, and behaviors induced by the syndrome are not part of a mental disorder, but rather the characteristic responses of a "reasonable" woman who has been brutalized by men in a male-dominated society.

BWS as a claim of self-defense challenges the current criminal law conception of self-defense, an idea based on masculine assumptions about human psychology. Charles Ewing examines the double standard inherent in the legal approach to self-defense. Specifically, he looks at the "no retreat rule," also known as the "true man rule," in which one is not required to retreat from an *imminent* threat of death or severe bodily injury, but may "stand one's ground and justifiably kill the attacker" (1990, 588). Although the law tries to discourage the unnecessary taking of a human life, it recognizes that making a *man* take on a cowardly, humiliating role is undesirable. By contrast, a woman is encouraged and expected to be "cowardly." In convicting battered women who kill, society's message is that "women are not supposed to use physical violence in self-protection; it is not our prerogative, our role, our right" (Osthoff 1992, 3). Concomitant to the gender-biased "true man rule" is the "castle doctrine," as in "every man's home is his castle." The "castle doctrine" claims that a person does not have to retreat when attacked or threatened with attack in *his* own home. Obviously, the castle doctrine has not been applied to women or such defenses as BWS would not exist in the first place. The sexist overtones are only too evident: a woman does not own a castle, she is part of the man's castle. Therefore she can't defend the castle—or herself in her own home.

It is important to note that the legal definition of "imminent" as specified in self-defense law "presupposes a one-time adversarial encounter." As such, Schneider observes, it "focuses on the circumstances immediately before the incident and does not take into account harm threatened in the past or future" (1980, 634). In 1988, Judy Norman was convicted of voluntary manslaughter and sentenced to six years imprisonment after she shot her husband in the back of the head while he was sleeping. Ms. Norman's story, like the stories of the women presented at the beginning of this chapter, involves over twenty years of severe physical, emotional, and psychological abuse: her husband slapped, kicked, and punched her on a continual basis; he treated her literally like a dog by forcing her to bark, to eat dog food, and to sleep on the concrete floor; he forced her to work as a prostitute to support the family while he himself did not usually work; and he threatened to "cut her heart out," among many other abominable acts (Tompkins 1993, 263–266). The State appealed Norman's conviction to the North Carolina Supreme Court and tried to persuade that court to allow the jury to receive instructions about the North Carolina law of self-defense. The state supreme court refused to permit such instruction and upheld the charge of voluntary manslaughter, ruling that the defendant was not in imminent danger because she was "not faced with an instantaneous choice between killing her husband or being killed or seriously injured" (Tompkins 1993, 266).

Yet this prompts one to ask, must the battered woman wait for her human time bomb of a batterer to explode before she is allowed to fight back? Subtle motions or threats by the batterer may not signify danger to an outsider, but "acquire added meaning for a battered woman whose survival depends on an intimate knowledge of her assailant" (Schneider 1980, 634). The law currently defines imminent danger as "presuppo[sing] a one-time adversarial encounter," and this severely narrow definition ensures that the battered woman will be at a disadvantage in any imminent situation. Furthermore, because the legal definition of imminent danger is so temporally specific, the delay between the abuser's assault and the battered woman's response can "render the immediacy of the threat questionable." The courts may thus decide to target the battered woman defendant's motivation as revenge rather than self-defense (Schuller & Vidmar 1992, 276).

"Why Didn't She Leave?": Separation Assault

Current legal definitions of imminent danger most often provoke the question, "Why didn't she leave?" If, indeed, there were a delay between the man's abuse and the woman's response, why didn't she just leave during that interval—while he was asleep, at work, or anywhere other than home? This question, the question most often asked of battered women who kill, naively assumes that leaving will stop the violence. On the contrary, the point of separation and the two years following is the most dangerous period in a violent relationship (Walker 1993, 246). At least half of the women who leave their abusers are followed and harassed or further assaulted by them (Mahoney 1991, 64). As noted in the Introduction, over 75% of battered women are single, separated or divorced, "with separated and divorced women facing the greatest risk of severe ongoing violence, including homicide" (Stark 1993, 667). Given these horrifying statistics, Martha Mahoney has argued for the recognition and enforcement of a specific criminal charge she calls "separation assault," defined as "the attack on the woman's body and volition in which her partner seeks to prevent her from leaving, retaliate for the separation, or force her to return" (Mahoney 1991, 65). According to Mahoney,

> The story of the violent pursuit of the separating woman must become part of the way we understand domestic violence to help eliminate the question "Why didn't she leave?" from our common vocabulary. . .the law assumes—pretends—the autonomy of women. Every legal case that discusses the question 'why didn't she leave?' implies that the woman *could* have left. (Mahoney 1990, 63–64)

Mahoney persuasively argues that separation assault must become a *formal* charge that can be used against the batterer. On a pragmatic level, separation assault is already recognized, as we can see from the existence of shelters and restraining orders. Although attacks on separated female partners are common, we cannot analyze this phenomenon until it has been named: "Naming separation assault has the potential to change consciousness in a manner comparable to the concept of 'date rape.' 'Date rape' and 'separation assault' name phenomena women know from our own experience, but which remain invisible without names" (Mahoney 1991, 68).

The concept of separation assault has not yet been tested. The recent passage of anti-stalking laws, however, may address this phenomenon. The anti-stalking law may be seen as the legislative equivalent to the restraining order, as it attempts to protect the battered woman by sequestering her from her abusive partner. Specifically, as Ann Jones notes, "Anti-stalking laws give police the power to arrest and detain stalkers, and courts the power to sentence them to substantial terms behind bars for the act of stalking itself, *before* the deadlier crime of assault or murder" (Jones 1994, 221; emphasis in original). Although there is some type of anti-stalking legislation in 48 states, this legislation is too recent to evaluate its effectiveness (Zorza 1995).

Treatment of the Batterer

In addition to pressing more specific charges against the batterer, many social scientists have suggested rehabilitating the batterer. Feminists have been wary of a therapeutic approach to battering because this approach tends to privatize and depoliticize the phenomenon. The most often cited studies of battering behavior (what we have been calling domestic violence against *women*) conducted by Murray Straus and Richard Gelles have been *gender-neutral*. In these studies, Straus and Gelles concluded that men and women abuse each other in equal numbers: they obtained these baffling and inaccurate results by weighing equally the violent behavior of hitting one's partner with a pillow to the hitting of one's partner with a sledgehammer (Jones 1994, 155). Until quite recently, most gendered studies have examined women's helplessness and passivity, instead of men's violence and aggression. Jones points to the recent trends in studying the men's behavior, but these studies are inconclusive because of inordinately high attrition rates (Jones 1994, 154; Gondalf 1993, 114; Hamberger and Hastings 1993, 190–194). Although some clinicians maintain that batterers do not share a definitive psychological profile, and that the most violent batterers may not be treatable, pro-feminist men have developed a consciousness-raising model for working with batterers. This model is based on the belief that "explanations for male violence toward women must include the political as well as the psychological dimensions of the problem" (Adams 1989, 69).

Simply put, men who batter have learned to use violence to control women. Their assumptions that violence towards and control over women are okay need to be challenged in order for any behavioral change to last.

A few studies show that the battering behavior *can* change if the batterer *completes* the court-ordered therapy (Pence and Shepard 1988, 288–290; Littleton 1989). In the majority of studies, however, determining success rates is difficult because few subjects participate in follow-up studies and because of the many methodological shortcomings in these studies (see Gondolf 1993; Hamberger and Hastings 1993). Furthermore, the outcome of batterer programs cannot simply be "compressed into some 'bottom line' intelligible to consumers—and investors" (Gondolf 1993, 114). Despite these discouraging observations, some researchers insist that batterer programs should continue, because such programs "reinforc[e] the individual efforts of some men to change their behavior" and they "present a visible symbol to the community that men can and should change" (Gondolf 1993, 107). As long as public and private funding remains limited, however, it seems that the more important investment should be made in programs and shelters for battered women: these women need a visible symbol from the community that they are valuable citizens who deserve protection and assistance.

Possible Solutions, Existing Limitations

Regrettably, there are no easy solutions to the problem of the conviction of battered women who kill their batterers. Osthoff advocates clemency for battered women as a short-term solution "[u]ntil the criminal justice system is free from the sexist notions that make it extraordinarily difficult for women who defend themselves to get a fair trial" (1992, 3). As proposed earlier, another solution may be to expand the current sexist and narrow definitions of imminent danger and self-defense; expanding these definitions would make a syndrome such as BWS unnecessary. Alternatively, Charles Ewing proposes a redefinition not of self-defense but of self. Despite overwhelming evidence that most women who kill are severely abused by the men they kill, many of these women are convicted because "the circumstances surrounding their homicidal acts do not meet the requirements of the current self-defense law—requirements that equate 'self' with only the physical aspects of personhood" (1990, 580). Advocating that the self be understood legally as it is commonly, Ewing argues that based on a common definition of the self, the psychological attributes are equal to, if not more important than, physical life and bodily integrity (586). Ewing specifies psychological attributes to include "security, autonomy, identity, consciousness, and spirituality" and bases this elaboration, in part, upon Laing's *The Divided Self: An Existential Study in Sanity and Madness*. In his evaluation of Ewing's argument, Stephen Morse attacks Ewing for applying vague existential philosophy to a legal definition of a distinct term. Ewing's concept of psychological self-defense has been used in courts only in conjunction with BWS, and its success—like the success of BWS—has been relatively minor (587–90). In a recent study of the effectiveness of Ewing's concept, mock jurists were as likely to convict (56%) as to acquit (44%) battered women defendants using psychological self-defense (Kasian 1993, 307). Other legal scholars suggest that expanding the definition of imminent danger might eliminate the need for a psychological self-defense (Roesch 1993, 294).

Until legal definitions are expanded to correspond to the realities of both men and women, however, using BWS as a defense is probably a battered woman's best bet. As one legal scholar has observed: "Rather than viewing the use of diminished capacity defenses [such as BWS] as repressive and a reflection of a sex-biased judiciary system, it can be argued that such pleas legitimize behavior that, under other circumstances, would be prohibited" (Kasian 1993, 310). Yet other legal scholars, as noted earlier, claim that framing a battered woman's reaction to violence as a syndrome or disorder (as in Post-Traumatic Stress Disorder) reinforces the myth of the helpless, hysterical, unstable woman. The argument that BWS perpetuates negative stereotypes of women is certainly a valid one. Yet such labels are preferable to a long prison term, at least in the interim.

Chapter 5

Feminists Negotiate The Legislative Branch: The Violence Against Women Act

Rachelle Brooks

> For too long, our society has looked the other way at this nightmare. It is shameful—but true—that our legal system condoned violence against—men for hundreds of years. And even now—for example, right here in Washington, D.C—an abusive spouse is arrested in less than 15 percent of the cases where his victim is *bleeding* from her open wounds. We cannot afford to wait any longer to treat domestic violence as...a serious crime. (Statement of Senator Joseph R. Biden, Jr., at Domestic Violence Hearing Before the Senate Judiciary Committee, December 11, 1990)

This chapter examines the most significant piece of legislation ever enacted on the subject of domestic violence against women, the Violence Against Women Act (VAWA), which was first introduced in the Senate in 1990, and was finally passed in 1994.[1] While other legislation in recent years has addressed the issue, none has offered as vast a package of grants, regulations, and guidelines directed at alleviating many forms of violence against women, including domestic violence. The reasons behind the initiation of the legislation are unclear. Senator Joseph Biden's (D-Del.) office drafted the legislation and introduced it to the Senate without offering specific reasons for deciding to take action on the issue. As the Act has moved through the legislative process, political and social circumstances have aided its progress. For example, public opinion on the issue of domestic violence has been a key factor in VAWA's success.

VAWA covers a variety of forms of violence committed against women, including rape and other forms of sexual assault, mugging and street violence, and violence committed on college and university campuses, as well as what has been defined as domestic violence against women. This section will present an overview of the legislation, giving special attention to the issue of domestic violence. The story behind this legislation's passage illuminates the many compromises and contradictions feminists faced in supporting this measure. While the law itself takes great steps toward achieving feminist goals on the issue of domestic violence, the *process* of negotiating the legislative branch proved to be much less straightforward.

Policy-making by Insiders and Outsiders

The legislative branch can successfully function as a location of feminist reform of public policy, despite the fact that all state and national legislatures are controlled by men, most of whom do not consider themselves feminists. There are two ways of achieving reform through legislation: women who hold elected office can work to enact legislation, and feminist lobbying groups can mobilize citizens and exert pressure for change. On the inside, women elected to legislatures are generally more liberal than their male counterparts in their policy positions and more interested in working on legislation which concerns women's rights, children, and families (Thomas 1994; Mezey 1994; Dodson and Carroll 1991). Therefore, their work *inside* the legislative branch is critical to reforming public policy. During the 1980s, outside feminist groups created lobbying organizations in Washington, D.C., in order to pressure lawmakers into addressing feminist concerns and to inform them of the impact various pieces of legislation would have on women (Costain and Costain 1987; Costain 1988; Walker 1991). This work by feminists on the *outside* has been crucial given the small number of feminists who have been elected to state or national legislatures.

Recent scholarship on women's activity in the legislative branch has largely focused on women in state legislatures, primarily because their greater numbers at the state level allow for more comprehensive and conclusive research. The overarching question these studies ask is: Do women make a difference in the legislature? In other words, does the presence of women result in different policies, approaches, behaviors, or priorities in statehouses? Several studies have concluded that women elected in the 1980s were very different from their male counterparts, in ways that had the potential for great impact on women in society:

> Research evidence over the last ten years supports the belief that many women politicians are different because they see things

> differently, because they understand the needs of women in society in a way that men cannot, and because many, if not most of them, will try to make the nation a better place for women and their families. (Mezey 1994, 256)

For example, women legislators are more likely to support progressive and feminist policy positions, and this finding holds for women legislators in both parties (Carroll, Dodson, and Mandel 1991). Sue Thomas asserts that these differences indicate that women have a distinct set of policy priorities which they work toward once elected:

> In short, women have gained latitude and experience in legislative politics to translate ideological stance, issue positions, and voting behavior into full fledged policy priorities. They have used these opportunities and have brought issues of women, and children and families into the center of their legislative efforts. (1994, 82)

In addition, they are as successful as men in enacting the legislation on which they work (Carroll et al. 1991).

However, in state legislatures where women make up a higher percentage of the overall membership, more priority legislation on women, children, and families is introduced, and women are more successful in the passage of their bills (Thomas 1994). This finding indicates that we should expect increasing numbers of bills dealing with feminist issues to be introduced and ultimately passed as more women permeate this branch of government.

Women are also active and successful working on feminist issues outside of the legislature. Over twenty years ago several feminist organizations established legislative offices in Washington, D.C. While at first achieving little success, they greatly expanded their influence in the mid-1980s. During this period national legislators became more concerned about their women constituents when a gender gap in voting behavior gained a great deal of attention (women voted slightly more Democratic than men). Organizations such as the National Women's Political Caucus and the Women's Equity Action League were thus able to capitalize on the gender gap and establish a women's lobby in Washington, D.C., which has continued to make headway and to gain strength[2] (Costain 1988).

In recent decades, lobbying has evolved into a massive institution in American politics. As one well-recognized scholar on interest groups commented: "Almost no important decision is made in Washington without the active, continuous involvement of some parts of the interest-group system" (Walker 1991, 1). In their attempts to influence the federal policy-making process, interest groups have proliferated in Washington, and it is unlikely that their presence will diminish in the foreseeable future. As a result, the presence of women's organizations and feminist lobbying groups in Washington has become a critical component of the process by which feminists can negotiate legislative policy-making.

The Existence of Federal Programs Before VAWA

Few federal programs and very little legislation addressed the problem of domestic violence against women before the introduction of the Violence Against Women Act. In 1977, two national domestic violence bills were defeated. However, feminists succeeded in attracting attention to the issue, and those in the battered women's movement continued to push for reform. In 1978, another large piece of legislation, the Domestic Violence Assistance Act, failed to pass. But the following year Democratic President Jimmy Carter established the Office of Domestic Violence with a budget of $900,000. Unfortunately in 1980 and 1981, with electoral success for the Republican party in the Senate and executive branch, more conservative ideology gained prominence. The New Right opposed domestic violence legislation, and President Ronald Reagan closed the Office of Domestic Violence in 1981. The Senate also took action against the Domestic Violence Prevention and Services Act and blocked its passage in 1980 (Pleck, 1987).

In 1984, the Family Violence Prevention and Services Act provided grants on a limited scale to support shelters, counseling, and related services for women and children who are victims of domestic violence. In addition, some grants for research and training for law enforcement agencies were also made available through this legislation. In fiscal year 1993, Congress allocated $24.8 million for the Act, with eighty-five percent of the money to be used for state-run programs.

The Victims of Crime Act of 1984 provides $150 million in grants to aid survivors of various crimes. The importance of this Act lies in the priority it gives to grants designed to assist victims of domestic violence, sexual assault, and child abuse.[3]

These early legislative successes are very tenuous because of competing partisan alliances and ideologies in Congress and the executive branch. The lack of a comprehensive piece of legislation on the national level made the Violence Against Women Act critical to women and feminists in Congress, and caused feminists activists and lobbying groups outside of Congress to organize quickly in support of the legislation.

Early Action on VAWA 1990-1991

On June 19, 1990, Senator Joseph R. Biden, Jr., introduced the first version of the Violence Against Women Act, and the Senate Judiciary Committee began hearings on the legislation the following day.[4] Introducing his legislation, Biden cited statistics compiled by the Justice Department which detailed the increasing rate of attacks on women each year.

In order for a proposed bill to become a law, it must travel through several channels. Each step is a potential stumbling block, yet allows for rigorous intervention by feminist lobbying groups and legislators. Upon being introduced in the House of Representatives or the Senate, a bill is referred to the appropriate committees for consideration. These committees are comprised of members of Congress, who then specialize in particular legislative areas. The committees often hold public hearings on the issues in proposed legislation. They must first approve the bill before they will pass it on to the floor for a vote by the full legislative body.

However, delays can take place at various points in the process. The committee may delay consideration of a bill, or it may reject part of the legislation and send it back for revisions before considering the rest of the bill. Once out of committee, the bill must be placed on the agenda so that the full House or Senate may vote on it. There are many reasons a vote may be delayed; if powerful members of Congress oppose the legislation, one of the biggest challenges may be just getting the bill on the agenda. These complicated lawmaking procedures demonstrate that the state may act in many incoherent ways which delay feminist initiatives, even without conscious, organized opposition.

In 1990, when the Judiciary Committee eventually considered the bill, survivors of violent attacks testified as to their experiences of judicial insensitivity, especially in connection with attempts to prosecute their attackers. Journalists were drawn to the issue, which resulted in a series of editorials and newspaper articles nationwide. The media focused on the victims of violent attacks, one of whom was a model before being slashed with a razor by an unknown attacker. The specific piece of legislation proposed to curtail the rate of domestic and sexual violence threatening women across the country was only discussed secondarily in many reports. It is likely that this media attention did a great deal to raise public awareness of domestic violence. The power of popular support is evidenced by the fact that the Judiciary Committee passed the bill unanimously on October 4, 1990. However, this did not guarantee swift action in making the bill a law. The full Senate did not vote on the bill, and Senator Biden reintroduced it in 1991.

In its original version, the bill had many components designed to assist survivors, to jail offenders, and to fund organizations working to combat violence against women. The first of its three sections, entitled "Safe Streets for Women," was intended to reduce the number of crimes against women perpetrated by strangers. It provided for disbursement of $300 million to law-enforcement agencies combating street crimes. The bill created the National Commission on Violent Crime Against Women, with the purpose of promoting national policy initiatives. The second section, "Safe Homes for Women," doubled the amount of federal funding for shelters and required interstate enforcement of court protective orders for women.

The third section originally introduced in the 1990 version of VAWA received the most attention from the media and women's groups. It designated sex crimes as "hate" crimes violating the civil rights of the victims, allowing them to seek compensatory and punitive damages under federal civil rights laws. Never before were crimes such as rape and battery allowed to be considered gender-motivated civil rights violations. Treating sex crimes as "hate" crimes meant that if a woman could prove that the violent act committed against her was an act motivated by hatred toward her because of her gender, she would be able to sue her attacker under federal civil rights law. Not only would attackers face prosecution under criminal code, but they would also face lawsuits from their victims under civil code. Crimes committed against people because of their race or religion are most commonly considered "hate" crimes. This was definitely the most controversial component of the bill, and a great deal of effort was expended throughout its movement through Congress to generate support for this section of the legislation.

On August 29, 1990, Senator Biden announced added provisions to the bill aimed at protecting young girls and women in schools. These additions were primarily aimed at college and university campuses and were designed to address the problem of date rape. However, they also expanded the purpose of the National Commission on Violent Crime Against Women to cover domestic violence as well as sexual assault. This meant that the Commission would also make policy recommendations about domestic violence issues and give domestic violence the national attention it deserves.

Unfortunately, this 1990 version of the Violence Against Women Act was not acted on by the full Senate, and was nullified as are all bills not passed before the session of Congress concludes. Therefore, the bill had to be reintroduced to the 102nd Congress in 1991, so that the process toward enactment could begin again.

There were few differences between the House and Senate versions of the Violence Against Women Act in 1990. Representative Barbara Boxer introduced the House version (H.R. 5468) and worked closely with Senator Biden. However, in 1990 the Senate bill was more comprehensive, especially in the area of domestic violence. Specifically, the Senate bill explicitly mentioned domestic violence as an area to be funded by the grants in the legislation. It also specified that domestic violence be included as a focus of the National Commission, whereas the House bill made no such provision.

Most of the action on the bill at this early stage was a result of hard work by insiders. Senator Biden held hearings on the bill to capture the attention of his colleagues and the media, so that he could begin to generate popular support for his initiative. However, action by interest groups was already beginning, and by 1991 they were prepared to take a more active role in support of VAWA.

Once again Senator Biden introduced to the Senate the Violence Against Women Act of 1991 on January 14, at which point it was referred to the Committee on the Judiciary. The new bill contained many technical changes in definitions, in the amounts of grants to be distributed, and in the requirements for receiving grants. These changes were likely due to the feminist activism around the issue, spearheaded by the National Organization for Women Legal Defense and Education Fund. This organization directed a task force of over 170 groups including unions, churches, and women's health and educational interest groups. The task force formed for the purposes of advising and lobbying Congress regarding revisions and additions to VAWA.

It was not until March 20, 1991, that the bill was reintroduced to the House by Representative Barbara Boxer (H.R. 1502). Two major differences existed between the bills in terms of domestic violence: (1) the Senate bill created programs in schools to educate children about domestic violence, while the House bill did not; (2) the Senate bill required commissions set up by states to study domestic violence, and authorized a national media campaign educating against domestic violence; these provisions were not in the House bill. In most other respects the two bills were virtually identical.

Throughout most of 1991, action by Congress on the bills was slow. By late in the year, components of the House bill had been added to other legislation. In the Senate, several attempts were made to attach VAWA to the crime bill; ultimately this did not happen. Unfortunately, a variety of other concerns preoccupied the supporters of VAWA, and Congress went into recess at the end of 1991, before it could seriously move the bill.

In 1991, action on the bill from the inside was slowed down by crowded agendas and shifting priorities of Members of Congress. However, the outsiders began to have significant influence on the legislation by organizing the Violence Against Women Task Force to lobby, make recommendations, and generate external pressure for VAWA.

The Final Stages 1992-1994

Throughout 1992, the bills in both the House and Senate continued to attract cosponsors. In October, Senator Biden held a press conference releasing the results of the Senate Judiciary Committee's research on violence against women. It is likely that Biden hoped to gain enough media attention to move the bill through Congress more swiftly during the next session. The lack of substantive action on the bill in the Senate throughout 1992 led Senator Biden to pledge to prioritize VAWA in 1993.

The scenario in the House was quite different. On September 23, the Crime and Criminal Justice Subcommittee, chaired by Representative Schumer (D-NY), held a mark-up of the bill. A mark-up is a line-by-line editing and revising process that each committee must undertake before releasing a bill. Several damaging amendments were attached to the bill in mark-up because key VAWA supporters on the subcommittee were not present.

On the positive side, by the end of 1992, the bill had gained a lot of publicity and attention. Organizational support was strong and momentum high as discussion began about who would reintroduce the bill to the next session of Congress, because Barbara Boxer had been elected to the Senate. Female Members of Congress were organized on the inside in support of VAWA, as evidenced by the preparations the Congressional Caucus for Women's Issues (CCWI) made to push the measure in 1993 *(Update*, 26

February 1993). This internal momentum was definitely needed to get the legislation moving.

On January 21, 1993, it was Senator Boxer herself, working with Senator Biden, who introduced VAWA, which became known as the Biden/Boxer bill; this bill was nearly identical to the 1992 Senate version. One month later in the House, the bill was introduced by Representatives Schroeder (D-CO), Slaughter (D-NY), Morella (R-MD), and Schumer (D-NY). Several new additions were included in the updated House version of the bill, including provisions for the protection of battered immigrant women. The Senate added a requirement that the Centers for Disease Control study the cost of domestic violence injuries. In addition, the Senate provided funding for a toll-free national hotline for victims of domestic violence.

The Senate Judiciary Committee unanimously approved VAWA on May 27, however not without several revisions and amendments; fortunately they did not radically change the bill. The next action on the bill in the Senate did not take place until November 19, when VAWA was attached to the Senate Crime Bill (H.R. 3355) which passed by a vote of 94-5 on that date. VAWA remained virtually intact, with only a few minor changes taking place in the process. An important omission in the Senate version was the lack of provisions to aid battered immigrant women (an important component of the House bill).

In the House, after months of waiting for any one of four subcommittees to take up the bill, activity occurred in November. On the 16th, the Judiciary Subcommittee on Civil and Constitutional Rights held a hearing on the civil rights provision of VAWA. On this same day, the House Judiciary Subcommittee on Crime and Criminal Justice voted to adopt a substitute bill. On November 17th, the full Judiciary Committee approved the bill and sent it to the floor of the House. Finally, on November 20, the House unanimously passed VAWA by a vote of 421-0. However, the bill had undergone a series of changes, including the elimination of the civil rights provision, because the Judiciary Committee claimed too little time had been allowed for hearings on this issue.

By the adjournment of Congress for winter recess at the end of the year, both the House and Senate had approved some version of VAWA. The upcoming challenge, and the final step towards making the bill a law, was for both sides to agree on one bill which would bridge the gulf between the competing versions.

Although the full House had passed a version of VAWA in 1993, it was decided that the VAWA measures should be incorporated into the Crime Bill in 1994, thus delaying the process once again. It was not until March 18, 1994, that the House Judiciary Committee passed a crime bill which included VAWA as Title XVI. Then, on April 21, the House crime bill was voted on and passed by the whole body of the House (285-141).

At this point the differences between the House and Senate versions of VAWA were vast. Specific measures in each of the bills were important, and the challenge for lobbying groups was to insure that the best parts of both bills ended up in the final version. Highlights of the differences, especially on the subject of domestic violence, included:

1. The Senate provided a greater allocation of funding overall for the programs, a total of $1.9 billion over five years. The House authorized only about $730 million over three years.
2. The House provided twice as much funding for a national domestic violence hotline ($1 million).
3. The House incorporated Native American Reservations and tribes into its provisions regarding the interstate enforcement of domestic violence laws.
4. The House bill prohibited the ownership of a gun by anyone convicted of domestic violence against an intimate partner or child under an order of protection.
5. The Senate stipulated that the Family Violence Prevention and Services Act address the needs of racial, cultural, and ethnic minorities.
6. The House bill had a total of five provisions designed to protect *immigrant* women from domestic violence, whereas the Senate bill had none.
7. The Senate bill provided $85 million for the Family Violence Prevention and Services Act, and an additional $400,000 for the development of programs to educate young people about domestic violence.
8. The Senate bill required that research on domestic violence be conducted by the Department of Justice and the Centers for Disease Control.
9. The Senate bill provided for prosecution under civil rights laws as a remedy for female victims of violent attacks.

(NOW LDEF, Side-by-Side Comparison, December 1993)

Now that VAWA had been incorporated into the Crime Bills in both houses of Congress, its fate would depend on bipartisan consensus on this complicated measure. Feminists on the outside were now faced with lobbying for a Crime Bill in order to get VAWA passed. Several measures in the Crime Bills were far from what many feminists would support to combat crime. For example, issues surrounding the death penalty, sentencing requirements, and community notification of the release of sex offenders were all included in the Crime Bills, and many of these approaches to crime are not ones most feminists can agree upon.

The Crime Bills also had several points of contention for Republicans and Democrats in Congress. A number of fundamental differences between the bills existed outside of the VAWA differences, and a bicameral committee had to sort them out before the final legislation could be sent to the president.

Three such discrepancies, which would dominate the debate on the measures for months to come, were the ban on assault weapons (included in the House bill), a Senate initiative to create a trust fund of $22.3 billion to pay for anti-crime programs, and a provision in the House bill which allowed for death row inmates to make an appeal on the basis that their sentence was racially discriminatory, commonly known as the Racial Justice Act (*Congressional Quarterly Weekly Report*, 23 April 1994, 1002–1003). Many of these issues were based in partisan politics, with Democrats supporting the gun ban and the Racial Justice Act, while Republicans opposed them. The House-Senate conference, which met for the first time on June 16, started work on a compromise of the trust fund issue, negotiating a $30 billion package over six years. However, disagreements over the Racial Justice Act snarled the committee work and postponed it until mid-July (*CQWR*, 25 June 1994, 1713).

Finally, on July 28, the committee approved a $33 billion crime measure (HR 3355), which included $1.8 billion for VAWA. The legislation also *included* a ban on semiautomatic assault weapons, but *eliminated* the Racial Justice Act. This created much opposition to the measure in both houses by gun rights advocates and the Congressional Black Caucus. This opposition would prove to be dangerous in attempting to gain enough floor votes to pass the final version of the Crime Bill in the House and Senate.

Some debate over VAWA also took place in the committee. Senator Biden strongly supported the provision which made gender-motivated crimes a civil rights violation. However, others viewed it as an unnecessary imposition on the federal courts, which would be required to hear the cases and decide if relief should be granted (*CQWR*, 30 July 1994, 2140). Ultimately, this provision was voted into the final version of the Crime Bill.

Success in 1994

On August 11, the full House gave consideration of the bill and blocked its movement by defeating the rule (210-225). Before any bill can be voted on, the rule, which sets guidelines for allowing debate and amendments to the bill, must reach agreement by a majority in the House. The vast majority of Republicans, along with eleven members of the Congressional Black Caucus, and many other Democrats, who were lobbied heavily by the National Rifle Association (NRA), voted against the rule. (The NRA was strongly opposed to the gun ban in the Crime Bill and encouraged Representatives to defeat the rule). The administration and Democrats in Congress considered this defeat to be particularly devastating. Without consensus on the rule, the bill cannot be voted on in the House, so it was then returned to the House-Senate committee for revisions.

On August 21, the House approved the revised version by a vote of 235-195. This version had come out of committee with $3.3 billion cut from its budget. On August 25, after a week of fierce debate and dissension, the Senate voted 61-38 to pass the bill exactly as it came out of committee, readying it for the President's signature. On September 13, 1994, President Clinton signed the Violent Crime Control and Law Enforcement Act of 1994, in which VAWA was enacted as Title IV.

In its final version, the $1.62 billion devoted to VAWA covers a wide range of programs to alleviate the abuse of women and children:

VAWA Provisions	*Allocation*[5]
Federal victim's counselors	$1,500,000
Training grants for law enforcement	800,000,000
Public transportation improvements	10,000,000
National park system improvements	10,000,000
Public parks improvements	15,000,000
Assistance to victims of sexual assault	205,000,000
Police training concerning sex offenders	2,000,000
Grants to reduce youth sexual abuse	30,000,000

Victims of child abuse programs	38,000,000
Training for judicial personnel	18,050,000
Televised testimony	4,250,000
Domestic violence hotline	3,000,000
Encouraging mandatory arrest programs	120,000,000
Battered women's shelters	325,000,000
Youth education on domestic violence	400,000
Community programs on domestic violence	10,000,000
State database study	200,000
CDC domestic violence	100,000
Rural domestic violence/child abuse	30,000,000
Education and training for state judges	600,000
Education and training for federal judges	700,000
Study on campus sexual assault	200,000
Stalker and domestic violence reduction	6,000,000
Total authorization over six years	$1,620,000,000

Two important provisions which remained in the final version of the Act do not deal with funding allocations. First is the Civil Rights Remedy for victims who can prove that the violence inflicted upon them was motivated by their gender. For example, under this remedy a victim may be awarded compensatory and punitive damages, as well as attorney's fees, if she successfully argues her case.

Secondly, the Act provides protections for battered immigrant women and children. These protections allow for some immigrants to petition for legal resident status and suspend the deportation of battered immigrant women when it would result in extreme hardship. Both of these provisions required strong lobbying efforts, both inside and outside, to ensure their inclusion in the final Crime Bill. The NOW LDEF Task Force pushed to have both of these measures included in the final bill. In addition, the Congressional Caucus for Women's Issues generated pressure when the Crime Bill was in conference to include these provisions (Carroll 1995).

The influences and pressures from both inside and outside the legislature were critical to the passage of VAWA and the larger Crime Bill. Feminist lobbying, individual women in Congress, and female members organized in the CCWI were all needed at different points in time to lead the bill through the maze of legislative politics. However, this case study also demonstrates the necessity of having support for a bill from the very highest levels of authority. Senator Joe Biden can be said to have had the greatest influence in the process, from the time the bill was first introduced to the final debates surrounding the Crime Bill. Without his work it is difficult to imagine what this legislation would look like, or if it would even exist. But the mobilization of women and feminist groups around him definitely granted a great deal of legitimacy to his legislation and exerted a degree of pressure which could not have been generated single-handedly.

By the end of the many debates surrounding the Crime Bill, it became readily apparent that public pressure forced Congress to take action and pass legislation that it may have been otherwise unwilling to agree upon. The Congressional elections in 1994 forced members of Congress to listen to their constituents, who continually said that crime was the most important issue affecting their lives. The Democratic defeats in the 1994 elections, and the resulting Republican control of both houses of Congress, led to a renewed discussion of the Crime Bill. Although discussions about reducing the amount of funding allocated to the bill took place as early as the first weeks Congress was in session for the new term, the VAWA provisions became an area which no one was willing to consider cutting. Perhaps this was because VAWA became a symbolic measure for members of Congress to offer as evidence of support for women's issues to their constituents.

Public opinion against domestic violence and other forms of violence against women may have also played a key role in the final preservation of VAWA. The O. J. Simpson murder trial, which began in 1994, brought to the public's attention the importance of addressing and alleviating domestic violence. In fact, it is possible that the case influenced Members of Congress during the final stages of discussion of the Crime Bill, discouraging cuts or amendments to VAWA (Carroll 1995). Legislators may hesitate to cut the funding of VAWA in the future, for fear that they will censured by their constituents at election time.

The Dilemmas and Deficiencies of Legislative Power

Undoubtedly, the Violence Against Women Act is an unprecedented move towards the alleviation of the domestic abuse women continue to face. VAWA has brought the attention of the media and national legislators to this problem, and has placed a women's issue on the national agenda. It has helped to insure that domestic violence is now a public issue, no longer left to the private affairs of family life. Although many other groups, such as children and the elderly, face domestic violence and will benefit from the legislation, the issue has been framed in terms of violence against women and thus attempts to incorporate as many of women's experiences as possible. In addition, the total amount of federal dollars being earmarked for programs which address domestic violence is truly unprecedented. While feminists and activists will debate who should receive the funds and which organizations should be given priority, the importance of this level of funding cannot be denied. However, several shortcomings in the Act serve as illustrations of the difficulties the legislative branch has in adequately serving the interests of women.

The fact that VAWA was ultimately consolidated into a crime bill placed many feminists in the awkward position of mobilizing around a measure with which they did not agree. Because feminist activists do not necessarily believe that the best approach to reducing crime includes longer jail terms or weapons bans (both of which were included in the Crime Bill), many were forced to compromise on these positions in order to accomplish their goal of getting VAWA passed. Furthermore, the symbolic act of consolidating VAWA in the Crime Bill means that the legislative system has grouped domestic violence with other violent crimes and has framed it as a criminal problem. By associating domestic violence against women with other criminal acts the state can ignore the many other roots of this violence.

As Chapter One explained, domestic violence has been treated historically at times as a social ill resulting from poverty or alcoholism. Related issues such as women's health or their economic vulnerability are also important for alleviating the problem and are not addressed by this legislation. For example, a law which proposed to address women's health concerns and included domestic violence in the measure would provide very different solutions to the problem. Likewise, if a law created greater economic equality for women, many would be better able to sustain themselves financially upon leaving an abusive relationship and would be less likely to return to their batterers. Other problems and paradoxes which many feminists see in attempting to use the police and other types of traditional crime-fighting mechanisms are discussed in more detail in Chapter Three. As long as domestic violence against women continues to be framed as a crime issue, the solutions the state can offer will necessarily be limited.

In other respects, too, the Crime Bill was a less than ideal piece of legislation around which feminist groups were forced to mobilize. For example, the fact that the Racial Justice Act was taken out of the crime bill further limited its sensitivity to women in minority communities. Feminists who supported the measure were forced to choose between a policy dealing with racism and a measure to alleviate the amount of violence committed against women. In supporting the final version of the crime bill feminists implicitly endorsed both the removal of the Racial Justice Act and what many consider to be inherent racism in our current system of justice. Domestic violence and racial justice issues became competing policies, rather than complementary ones, thus exemplifying the frequent inability of the state to address women's and feminists' multiple allegiances and identities. In addition, VAWA only occasionally addresses problems which may be unique to women of color or poor women, and the problems of abuse lesbian women face were largely absent from the debates. By ignoring the specificity of women's circumstances, the Act itself creates gaps through which many women will fall.

Furthermore, several shortcomings of the VAWA civil rights provision limit its applicability. While at face value the inclusion of gender-motivated hate crimes under civil rights law is valuable, it has several theoretical and practical shortcomings. Some would argue that all violence women encounter is a result of sexism and a violation of women's civil rights, while others would contend that an explicit statement by the perpetrator against women as a class would be necessary for the victim to receive a remedy under civil rights law. At this point the dilemmas feminists face when engaging the state become all too apparent. If the law and the state do not recognize the pervasiveness of sexism in society, pursuing a civil rights claim will be very difficult for most women. In fact, domestic violence cases probably would not be eligible for remedies under civil rights law. Additionally, what sort of claim might a lesbian Latina woman who is raped pursue? Was this a hate crime based on her gender, her race, or her sexual orientation? Would it be considered a hate crime at all if the rapist never made reference to her gender, race, or orientation?

These shortcomings of VAWA exemplify only a few of the problems and paradoxes feminists face when working with the state to alleviate domestic and other types of violence against women. As we use the state to address our grievances, we must also force it to reconsider and redefine its classification schemes, so that multiple solutions to problems are addressed and all women benefit equally from state resources.

Several conclusions can be drawn from this review of the Violence Against Women Act. First, the media and public opinion played an important role throughout its progress in becoming a law. Because Members of Congress are directly accountable to their constituents through the election process, they often monitor the public's attitudes and sentiments.

In the case of VAWA, feminists were not critical in mobilizing public opinion, as described earlier in Chapter One. Instead, this was done by the Senators who sponsored the bill and by social and political circumstances external to this piece of legislation. However, the political opportunity created by public opinion is definitely necessary for success in using the state.

Secondly, tradeoffs are necessary even when the best of intentions are motivating state actions. The insider legislators who were active around VAWA were very open to suggestions from outsider activists and lobbyists, and were willing to incorporate many of their ideas into the legislation to make it more inclusive and comprehensive. Specifically, the fact that the provisions for immigrant women remained in VAWA is a tribute to the dedication of feminist groups who were unwilling to compromise and exerted pressure on legislators. Ultimately, however, feminists were in the position of mobilizing around a Crime Bill in order to address violence against women. That compromises by feminists were critical in some instances, even as they could hold their ground at other times, demonstrates that negotiation with the state is possible, but requires a careful and in-depth understanding of its processes by feminists.

Chapter 6

Feminist Strategies: The Terms of Negotiation

The Collective

Societies both regulate and protect their members. In a democratic society, decisions about who needs protection from what, how much regulation is needed, and who bears the burden of regulating are continually negotiated within a context of changing power relations and public concerns. Intrusive regulation can in fact be a form of "repressive benevolence." At the same time, lack of protection, as the history of domestic violence illustrates, conveys the indifference of those in power towards the abuse and exploitation of less powerful groups. Neither extreme is acceptable. A major goal of this project is to bring about a more just balance between the protective and regulatory functions of the state. This requires that we interrogate the ways in which both the state's actions and inactions privilege and penalize citizens in accord with gender, class and race inequality.

In demanding equality and protection for women, feminists addressing domestic violence have engaged the three branches of government in specific ways, with specific agendas. Feminists hold the state accountable because it reproduces the conditions that perpetuate domestic violence—the practices that foster these conditions must change. In addition, feminists petition the state for resources they need in order to pursue both the immediate work of protecting women and the long-term projects of preventing and ultimately ending domestic violence. These resources include funding for organizations and programs and official recognition of their work. Without some recognition from the state as legitimate agents working on behalf of battered women, feminists have little credibility or influence in the social welfare and criminal justice arenas.

Feminists have found that remedies offered by the state for domestic violence are complex and often insufficient. The executive branch, the courts, and the legislature all too often reinforce the underlying causes of women's victimization, even as they attempt to alleviate or deter domestic violence. It is this paradoxical function of state power that complicates the use of the state for feminist ends. As a result, feminist goals must be sought both within the boundaries of formal state authority, as well as outside of its sphere in independent, community-based activism.

In negotiating for changes in the practices, resources and authority of state institutions, feminists make compromises. The state frames issues according to what it can most easily accommodate within existing structures. Constraints on feminist engagement include the state's commitment to the current gender order and its ability to co-opt the less radical aspects of the reform agenda.

In this process of engagement, feminists must clearly and consistently articulate a bottom line—an immutable set of principles which guide negotiations with the state. We believe this bottom line must be constituted by two fundamental rights, without which all women will remain second-class citizens. These are the right to economic security and the right to be free from the threat of violence. Unfortunately, neither economic nor physical security are realities for women. Fifty percent of the women and children living on the street are escaping domestic violence.[1] In New York City between 1990 and 1994, nearly half of women's killers were current or former husbands or boyfriends (Belluck 1997). Women continue to be segregated into the lowest paying jobs and to juggle the responsibilities of children and waged work without significant help from the government or employers. Women have historically fought for the right to vote, to own property, and to work. Women must now also demand the rights to economic and physical security. Ultimately, our goal cannot be limited to the integration of women into formal political rights, but must include the transformation of citizenship to address the specific needs of women. We must move beyond the state's protection of women as second-class citizens, towards women's physical, emotional, and economic empowerment.

In the following sections, we identify feminist accomplishments, review the constraints faced in negotiation with the state, and consider the ways in which these constraints have shaped the outcomes of engagement. What are the resulting trade-offs and sacrifices in this process of ongoing negotiation? We also categorize and evaluate feminists' accomplishments according to the bottom line issues of women's physical and economic security. To what extent have negotiations with the state achieved, or fallen short of, the goals central to women's long-term empowerment?

Principles of Negotiation

One purpose of our project has been to document the ways in which feminists have succeeded in placing domestic violence on the national political agenda. Feminist successes are evident in the widespread acceptance of an empowerment model for assisting battered women, the coordination of a national movement addressing domestic violence, the recognition of violence against women in intimate relationships as a public issue, the criminalization of domestic violence, the establishment of grounds for the defense of women charged with murdering men who battered them, and the passage of the Violence Against Women Act. These successes are interrelated; they overlap in chronology and substance.

Yet the constraints of negotiating with a state that is run predominantly by men and in men's interests tempers these accomplishments. We characterize this as the "gendered state" (see Appendix) in order to capture the dynamic process by which feminists confront and challenge governmental power. While specific to negotiations over domestic violence, our study of feminist state activism suggests broader insights into this process of negotiation for all feminist efforts directed at the state. We now turn to an examination of these.

The state is not enough. Activism within the state must always be balanced by the activism of women's independent community-based organizations.

The history of the battered women's shelter movement provides a good illustration of the paradoxes faced by community organizations as they both maintain independence from state bureaucracies and draw upon the resources of the state for women's immediate protection.

The shelter movement created a space in which battered women and activists (both professional and grass-roots) engaged in collective analysis and consciousness-raising. The shelters provided refuge for battered women, making it possible to see the large numbers of women who experienced and sought to leave abusive marriages. At the same time, they were essential bases for organizing and advocating. While many different types of women's groups experimented with collective decision-making and non-hierarchical leadership, the more radical shelters became models of women-run communities. In these communities, residents engaged in their own decision-making and problem-solving activities and received group support. The general feminist model for assisting battered women still emphasizes safety, support, and practical help with future plans rather than psychological or therapeutic treatment.

Shelters as residential communities suggested an alternative to marriage and the nuclear family and also demonstrated the viability of institutions run by women. They presented a challenge to the prevailing gender order based on heterosexual relationships and women's dependency on men. In response to this challenge, attempts were made to discredit the shelters. Battered women's advocates were characterized as lesbians who were trying to steal women from their husbands[2] (Bako 1980). Such tactics succeeded, and lesbians became less visible in the shelter movement. Another tactic to counteract the radical influence of shelters was to establish non-feminist programs for domestic violence under the auspices of mainstream institutions.

Feminist shelters experienced pressure to conform to prevailing organizational norms in order to secure funding and win public trust as the programs best able to respond to domestic violence. Responses to this pressure included resistance, creative compromise, and bureaucratic capitulation.[3] What the shelter movement gained through integration into the social welfare funding arena was offset to some extent by decreased freedom to experiment with innovative structures and loss of opportunities to understand heterosexist systems from the lesbian vantage point. Many programs, however, did not lose sight of the changes in gender relations necessary for long-term change, and some shelters continued to include anti-homophobic education as part of their work, or began such education after becoming well-established (Cagan 1992; Reinelt 1995).

Networks established among shelters were essential to coordinate organizing, lobbying, and public education efforts. Shelters formed the foundation for statewide coalitions and a national organization, the National Coalition Against Domestic Violence (Reinelt 1995). During the 1980s, when shelters were integrated into large networks serving crime victims, feminist programs maintained some autonomy and exercised some leadership because of their record of successful work with battered women.

Establishing shelters has been one of the major feminist strategies to protect battered women. However, the vision of early activists in the shelter movement was not limited to establishing an adequate number of refuges. Shelters provided needed protection, but their function as alternative, experimental communities and as sites for consciousness-raising and organizing were equally important.

The state accommodated the protective function of shelters. State bureaucracy subsumed shelters and their programs, enabling feminists to continue to exert political influence as part of the state infrastructure (Reinelt 1995). Yet the state's enthusiastic response to the demand for battered women's shelters demonstrates how a short-term goal can become a permanent solution. The need for fundamental change may be felt less urgently because the state has demonstrated its willingness to evacuate battered women from their homes indefinitely.

The power to "name and frame" issues is as important as (and essential to) accessing the material resources of the state. Issues must be framed in language and ideological terms consistent with women's empowerment.

A necessary part of any system of oppression is an ideology supporting that oppression (Adams 1989). In order to make violence against women visible and keep the focus on male violence as the problem, we need to recognize the ways in which power and gender ideology are used to name and define social problems.

Our society takes for granted the socially constructed categories of private life and personal problems. Although domestic violence against women affects a large population, it has only recently been defined as a social or public problem. For most of our country's history, families and intimate relationships belonged to the realm labeled private and personal. Our society also values individual freedom, making it difficult to perceive the ways in which groups with greater power and privilege systematically maintain their advantage at the expense of other groups. In other words, emphasis on the individual detracts from identifying widespread group-based or structural problems.

The production of knowledge about domestic violence against women is tainted with cultural beliefs about gender. Feminists must challenge the ideas used to minimize or dismiss male violence against female partners. Examples of such ideas are: "many couples fight"(gender neutrality), "don't interfere, it's a private matter" (sanctity of the private home), and "if she doesn't leave, she's just asking for it" (individual responsibility). Feminists have successfully analyzed the ways these concepts are used and have formulated a coherent framework for understanding domestic violence as a social, gendered phenomenon rooted in family and marital law, social welfare policy, the economic system, and the labor market.

In their efforts to protect and empower women and to show why gender relations need to change, feminists constantly negotiate the terms for defining, studying, and intervening in domestic violence as they interact with the many facets of the state and with the public. For example, in the social science arena, feminists dispute the notion that battered women's situations are adequately addressed by the concept of "family violence"—an overbroad gender neutral label that obscures the prevalence of male violence against female partners (married or unmarried) and includes other phenomena like child or elder abuse. In the mental health system, feminists pointed out that therapists often ignored the impact of male violence on their female clients. When psychiatrists did acknowledge male violence, feminists had to launch a campaign to prevent them from creating a new diagnostic category for women in abusive relationships, Self-Defeating Personality Disorder (Herman 1992).

Defending battered women who kill their batterers is now based on the notion that experiencing battering over a period of time causes a psychological syndrome. Again, the syndrome frames the situation in terms of individual responsibility, and argues that because of the effects of battering on her mental state, a particular woman was not able to act responsibly in the "normal" way. The criminal justice system has accepted Battered Woman's Syndrome because it does not challenge prevailing gender ideology. It does not specify that the source of the problem is the man's violence or the failure of the state to protect women from violent men. While Battered Woman's Syndrome has worked to keep some women out of jail, it has categorized them as mentally unstable and has reinforced stereotypes about women's health and sanity. This is a good example of framing a social issue in terms that undermine the long-term goal of empowering women.

Current efforts to expand the definition of self-defense to include actions taken by women who know their lives are in imminent danger provide an alternative strategy. The law and definitions or interpretations of the law need to be redesigned or expanded to reflect women's experiences, realities, and needs as well as men's. As we suggest, one approach is to claim that women have the right to be free from the threat of bodily harm. Another approach is to classify acts of violence against women as hate crimes and give women access to civil as well as criminal procedures for penalizing offenders.

The short-term goal of women's immediate protection must not undermine the long-term goal of women's empowerment.

Women's protection should not come at the cost of legitimating a masculine culture of violence in the police and criminal justice systems. Public, legitimate, and presumably benevolent forms of male violence cannot be used to prevent private, illegitimate, and malevolent male violence in the home.

Controversies over mandatory arrest policies provide a good example of the ways in which even the most radical short-term reforms may undermine the longer-term goals of gender and racial equity. Feminists have legitimately expected that criminalizing domestic violence would provide some immediate protection to women in the greatest danger and also decrease the incidence of battering. However, because the state acts to accommodate demands without disrupting existing gender, racial, and class structures, we find that the police who carry out a pro-arrest policy in domestic violence situations still bring sexist, racist, and homophobic attitudes with them. They are not likely to be regarded as sources of help in many communities.

Feminists have substantially, although not unanimously, supported mandatory arrest policies. One of the undesirable outcomes of mandatory arrest has been an increase in the arrests of women. Another outcome has been jeopardizing feminists' potential coalitions with groups in poor communities or communities of color that prefer to address domestic violence without police intervention.

Those feminists who believe that mandatory arrest establishes a new social norm for male behavior may be willing to make these sacrifices. Yet one dramatic change in the law cannot bring about a profound change in social attitudes and behaviors. The problem remains that changing the law does not, in itself, change the social structure.

Because recognition of the roots of domestic violence and the legal and economic barriers battered women face cannot be built into a law, enforcement of the law can still occur in a discriminatory fashion. Only when more basic elements of the criminal justice system are transformed can we begin to realize the potential for long-term changes that would meet battered women's needs and decrease institutional support for male violence against women. Battered women's advocates have shifted the attention of the criminal justice system from how the battered woman can help the system prosecute her case to how its resources may be used to prevent violence and help women pursue their goals for the future.

The dominance of men, sexist practices, and sexist ideology in the criminal justice system need to be challenged as well. Three levels of strategy with the police are called for, and they may be difficult to pursue simultaneously. Some battered women's advocates feel that rewarding the police for aggressively responding to the batterer's crime is the most effective way to protect battered women. Yet feminists must also fight to integrate more women into the police force and support the demands of minority and poor communities for responsible, respectful police behavior and for better representation on the police force.

Efforts to address domestic violence must be connected to advocacy for racial and class equality, as the foundation for building more effective broad-based political coalitions.

We have suggested that feminists engaging with the state are often confronted with a series of trade-offs and sacrifices. The history of the

American women's movement suggests that leading feminist organizations have often compromised the needs of poor women and women of color in order to win the state's support for more moderate political reform. Advocates addressing domestic violence must not strike this compromise.

Lobbying for the Violence Against Women Act illustrates the problems associated with slighting poor women and women of color in efforts to achieve legislative success. The Violence Against Women Act used mainstream language to gain popular and legislative support. As a result, it did not address the ways violence affects women of color or the larger connections between poverty, crime, and violence experienced by women living in poor communities. The failure to address the connections between economic insecurity and violence against women affects not only women of color and poor women, but all women— working class, middle class, and upper class—who continue to stay in violent relationships for economic reasons.

Feminists can build broad-based coalitions to link violence against women to violence in inner-city communities. Domestic violence policy must also be linked to issues of central concern to poor communities, including employment and welfare policies and police and criminal justice issues.

The activism of outsiders must be linked to the power of insiders in all three branches of government.

Women's issues have increasingly gained visibility within the political process as more feminists have entered the executive, judicial, and legislative branches of government. Yet for feminist insiders to be effective, they must reflect and be responsible to the concerns of women who remain outside governmental power. Efforts to pass the Violence Against Women Act illustrate the effectiveness of linking outside lobbying with the power of influential legislators. Historically, feminists have organized more effectively to influence the legislative branch of government than either the executive or judicial branch. To negotiate the legislative process many feminist groups have formed with the express purpose of lobbying. Compromises that feminists make are most visible in negotiation with this branch of government, because compromise is built into the legislative process.

Yet even when we look at the judicial and executive branches of government, we see the significance of the influence of women who have positions of state power. Police departments are more likely to respond effectively to calls from abused women if women have been integrated into the police force. Judges who are female are more likely to deliver just punishment to abusers. In 1990, women held 13% of the jobs on the police force (including detectives), while women made up 27% of lawyers and judges (Roberts 1995). The percentage of women in the police force has doubled since 1970, while the percentage of women who are lawyers and judges has quadrupled.

While neither the police force nor the judicial system can be considered highly accessible or open to change, women's rapidly increasing representation in district attorneys' offices, in law firms specializing in women's issues, and in judgeships suggest that feminists may have more inside help in the courtroom. In addition, police actions are often criticized and the public often holds local elected officials accountable for the actions of the police.

Feminists have successfully used law suits, publicity, and political pressure to hold the police accountable for their failure to enforce the law in domestic violence situations. Although the police have resisted, for a number of reasons, identifying as criminal the behavior of men who assault their female partners, the current trend to insist that they do so is not likely to reverse (Jaffe, Hastings, Reitzel, and Austin 1993). New Jersey's Prevention of Domestic Violence Act of 1991[4] demonstrates the deliberateness with which state legislatures have criminalized domestic violence:

> The Legislature finds and declares that domestic violence is a serious crime against society: The Legislature further finds and declares that even though many of the existing criminal statutes are applicable to acts of domestic violence, previous societal attitudes concerning domestic violence have affected the response of our law enforcement and judicial systems, resulting in these acts receiving different treatment from similar crimes when they occur in a domestic context...It is further intended that the official response to domestic violence shall communicate the attitude that violent behavior will not be excused or tolerated, and shall make clear the fact that the existing criminal laws and civil remedies created under this act will be enforced without regard to the fact that the violence grows out of a domestic situation. (New Jersey Code of Criminal Justice: 2C:25-18[5])

While the power of insiders is critical to political success, we caution against too much of a "top-down" approach: the initiatives of those within state government must be based upon the needs and concerns of women in their communities.

The political agenda must be expanded to set domestic violence in the context of a wide range of gender equity issues.

It is crucial to recognize the ways in which domestic violence is deeply connected to other forms of gender inequality and to expand the political agenda to address the full range of causes of violence and the full range of solutions needed to empower women in abusive relationships. Now that feminist-oriented educational programs have made it impossible to maintain specific victim-blaming myths, such as "women enjoy being beaten" or "women provoke their husbands' violence," the tactic for sweeping the problem of domestic violence under the rug has become simply to ask, "Why doesn't she leave?" One wonders how this question can be taken so seriously when new battered women's shelters immediately fill to capacity. Yet feminists attempt to answer the question, drawing on their understanding of many factors affecting women who remain with or return to abusive men.

Battered women may be emotionally dependent on the batterer, they may be afraid that the batterer will become even more violent towards them if they leave, and they may feel it would be wrong to "break up the family." Perhaps most importantly, single mothers are legally and economically disadvantaged in this society; segregation in the low-wage sector of the labor market, inequitable pay, and lack of good, affordable child care prevent many women from being able to achieve financial independence. If women leave their children in order to escape from violence, they have little chance of re-establishing any parental rights in the future. Finally, women who leave are most at risk for being hurt or killed.

Providing money for battered women's shelters or requiring the police to arrest batterers on sight may temporarily eliminate the immediate threat of violence. However, the long-term problems women face when they leave a violent relationship are rarely considered in the making of public policy. Job training, child care, affordable permanent housing, legal assistance, and health care on a continuing basis are only some of the needs survivors of domestic abuse may have. The state rarely considers these issues to be critical when it attempts to find solutions to the problem of domestic violence, and thus it has provided only limited, inadequate relief measures.

Yet it is important to ensure that domestic violence not be politically submerged under other political agendas, such as general crime reduction. The fact that sexual harassment, rape, and domestic violence are grouped together under the Violence Against Women Act has great symbolic value —the gendered nature of these crimes is acknowledged. However, this historic legislative response to violence against women is included in a crime bill that assumes our criminal justice system to be neutral, benevolent, and able to address the problem, albeit with some tinkering around the edges. Combined with VAWA's lack of attention to improving women's economic independence, this assumption may limit the ability of the act to lead to significant long-term change.

Although VAWA began as a distinct piece of legislation, it was ultimately enacted as one section of a much larger crime bill. This allows members of Congress and others who will enforce the legislation to continue to conceive of domestic violence as a law and order issue. This is also how the problem tends to be characterized by the general public. However, stopping the battering of women will require much more than additional dollars for shelters and sensitivity training for police and court personnel. It will require eliminating the reasons men believe they can and should abuse their intimate partners. And these reasons have very little to do with crime and are much more closely related to our system of gender ideology.

By connecting activism around domestic violence with activism on other gender equity issues, we reveal how intimate violence is produced by a larger system of gender inequality that reinforces the idea that women are the private possession of men. We also acknowledge the connections between the devaluation of women's work and worth in the public sphere with their abuse at home.

In confronting the paradox of state power, feminist activism must advocate women's empowerment. This empowerment can only be achieved once women have gained the twin rights of economic and physical security. Only women who are free from the threat of destitution are truly free to leave abusive relationships. Only women who are free from the threat of physical violence can be said to be full and equal citizens. For what does it mean to be a citizen if the state's resources are not used to prevent physical abuse, or if the state fails to seriously punish those responsible for the abuse? For women, physical and economic security go hand and hand. This must be the vision with which feminists confront the state.

Appendix

Feminists and the State: A Theoretical Exploration

Sandra Marshall

Feminist activists often find the possibility of mobilizing the state to address inequalities and abuses in society that affect women, like domestic violence, necessary because of the vast power and resources the state commands. Yet the state historically has failed to take violence against women seriously and has, in fact, contributed to a broader cultural acceptance of masculine violence. For example, the state both teaches men to be violent through military training and punishes men for violent behavior. From this perspective it can seem more effective to pursue other avenues of social change, such as constructing alternative institutions to mediate crises. Battered women's shelters are an example of this.

Arguably, the best solution is for activists to combine both approaches. Feminists can engage the state as effectively as possible while also pursuing other solutions. Theoretical clarity, focused upon the complexities and paradoxes of the state, can assist feminists with state interactions.

Defining the State

"The state" as a concept is clearly too broad to allow a simple definition. An elementary definition casts the state as comprised of elected and administrative governmental institutions, both at the local and national levels (Hernes 1992, 75). Such a definition evokes familiar images of government officials and easily recognizable state functions, such as mail delivery and foreign policy actions. Yet the simplicity of the definition can also be limiting.

German philosopher, Max Weber, offered what has since become a classic definition of the state as a human community that has successfully claimed a monopoly over the legitimate use of force within a given territory

German philosopher, Max Weber, offered what has since become a classic definition of the state as a human community that has successfully claimed a monopoly over the legitimate use of force within a given territory (Weber 1958, 77–78). Thus Weber casts the legitimate use of violence as the sole defining characteristic of the state.

A contradiction emerges when feminists look closely at Weber's definition. In practice, individual men can commit a great deal of violence against women without suffering any consequences; this, of course, is one of the main problems with domestic violence. Furthermore, it can be argued that the state legitimates this violence by not taking effective action to stop it. The reality of this violence compromises Weber's conception of the state as holding a monopoly over legitimate coercion (Walby 1990, 150).

In addition to defining the state in terms of institutions and force, many theorists also include a view of society characterized by competing and conflicting interests. The idea of interests helps to define the state in terms of its role as a regulator of or arena for political interests; the liberal and Marxist approaches to the state expand this formulation. The efforts of special interest groups to influence government policy underscores this function of the state. In general, however, accounts of the state include a view of the state as a centralized institution, perceive that force underpins the powers of the state, and frame the state as a site where political interests can compete (Walby 1990, 150).

In response to the empirical and theoretical complexity of the state, some modern state theorists have begun taking another approach. The state's extreme complexity and enormous size, as well as its ever expanding power, has rendered it increasingly difficult to construct empirical boundaries around the state in order to define it. Instead, modern theorists frequently conceptualize the state as a process rather than as an objective entity. Such a framework allows theorists to explore the ways in which the state regulates society and to develop a more subtle conception of state power. In addition, a process of internal coordination is necessary to ensure that the actions of the state possess some degree of coherence in practice. A theoretical focus upon this aspect of the state is particularly relevant in analyses of bureaucracy (Connell 1994, 138). This approach is particularly useful for feminist theorists.

These general definitions demonstrate that the complexity of the state quickly emerges within theoretical analyses. It is this complexity that demands theoretical clarity by feminists who engage the state in efforts to effect social change. The following sections explore the major theoretical frameworks which have been used in analyses of governmental power.

Liberalism and Liberal Feminism

Liberalism conceives of the state as a neutral arbiter of competing interests. Citizenship grants the right of access to the state, or the right to assist in the formulation of state policy. Although liberalism posits the state as neutral, it recognizes that the process may be biased. However, because the government is a site for competing interests, it also allows struggles to take place which strive for the ideal of neutrality (Franzway, Court, and Connell 1989, 14).

Liberal feminists use the progressive liberal conception of the state as a social arbiter for the basic framework within which to develop strategy. Liberalism does not assume that the state is necessarily neutral, only that it should be. Thus liberal feminists argue that the state is not neutral in its treatment of women, they perceive the state as being dominated by men, and they define the problem of sexism as one of imperfect citizenship (Franzway, Court, and Connell 1989, 14). As a result, the analyses of liberal feminists often emphasize the fact that women are largely absent from powerful positions within state structures and from formal political elites. Because the underlying assumption is of a neutral state, liberal feminists usually argue that the presence of more women in positions of authority would result in state policies that are more favorable towards women (Walby 1990, 151–153). The efforts by groups such as the National Organization for Women to increase the number of women holding elected political office serve as an example of liberal feminist strategy.

The politics of liberal feminism historically have been quite successful. The feminist activists fighting for suffrage utilized a liberal understanding of citizenship to justify women's right to vote. More recently, the increased access of women to welfare services, equal opportunity programs, and the anti-discrimination laws and cases all owe debts to liberal feminists. Furthermore, the greater numbers of women holding state offices are partially a result of the liberal feminist emphasis upon equal access to the public arena (Franzway, Court, and Connell 1989, 14–15).

Attempts to change the police, the courts, and the laws in relation to domestic violence draw several theoretical conceptions from liberal feminism. The idea that women have a right to protection from violence emerges from the liberal conception of the rights of citizens. In addition, the assumption that the state is neutral, or can be made neutral, supports feminist efforts to change state institutions and policy. Liberal feminists argue that training the police or passing laws that punish batterers will be effective, because the state itself is neutral and thus not structurally implicated in domestic violence.

Liberal feminism also provides a potentially fertile theoretical ground for strategies that take into account differences among women. Because poor women and women of color have basic rights denied to them, the feminist fight to ensure full citizenship rights to all women can continue to effect dramatic changes in the lives of all women (see Eisenstein 1994). Feminist awareness of such differences is particularly important in relation to domestic violence, as state policies can have profoundly different effects on women in varied situations.

There are, however, important limitations to the liberal feminist approach. Some feminists point to the essential conflict within the ideology of liberalism, which is the conflict between individual freedom and structural inequality (Eisenstein 1984, 87). Because liberalism allows for structural economic inequality, freedom for all individuals is ultimately limited. Societal inequalities restrict the ability of many people to exercise their freedom to compete. Furthermore, it is not a fully legitimate function of the liberal state to take actions that address inequalities. This helps to explain the backlash against women and the advances made by the women's movement.

There are other problems with liberalism. Because liberalism posits a neutral, or ideally neutral, state, the result is a conception of the state as above and removed from the social conflicts below. The state regulates public life, yet is separate from the private realm. More specifically, the state is seen as separate from the social contexts that foster domestic violence. In contrast to this view, other feminist perspectives argue that the state is actually part of social conflicts. State activities emerge from these conflicts, primarily because the state is committed to mediating conflicts and creating order (Eisenstein 1981, 225). Such a view of the state is elaborated upon in the discussion on Marxism below.

In addition to these specific criticisms of liberal feminism, a more general yet important drawback to this perspective relates to its theoretical weaknesses. The liberal feminist conception of the state is essentially rootless theoretically, a problem further compounded by a lack of a social theory regarding gender. Liberal feminists approach the current system of male dominance as a historical accident and create strategies that suggest reform is the solution. From this perspective, programs such as affirmative action and the removal of sex role stereotypes within the educational system are thought to change attitudes, thus bringing to an end the reasons for unequal citizenship. The result would thus be the properly neutral state (Franzway, Court, and Connell 1989, 15). Yet the recent history of the women's movement illustrates that the solution is not that simple.

It can be argued that the political effectiveness of liberal feminism is ultimately limited by its lack of a developed theory of the state. Although this approach appears to be restricted to effecting reforms, feminist theorists continue to produce innovative work within liberal feminism (see Ackelsberg 1988 and Jones 1990). Such work suggests that liberal feminism continues to be useful, though limited, as a practical framework for strategy.

The Public/Private Split

Because the United States is a liberal political system, the conception of separate public and private realms is imbedded in the law and doctrines concerning the state's relationship to the family. Issues surrounding the public and private realms become particularly salient in relation to domestic violence, as this violence occurs in the private realm, a place ideologically separate from the state. However, feminist theorists question this vision of the private.

Within the liberal framework, the state should be not only neutral, but ideally confined to the public sphere. Theoretically, the state does not determine what occurs in private life. Feminists have argued that the private sphere is both defined by and regulated in relation to the state realm. The state constructs and protects the division between public and private (Eisenstein 1984, 89). The state's interest in the family and how family is defined, although obscured by the official doctrine concerning the public/private split, cannot be ignored by feminists confronting domestic violence. From this perspective, the issue is not should the state intervene in the private sphere, but how this intervention should occur. The feminist movement, as it made the issue of private violence one of public debate, has also revealed that state interference in the family is not a new development, but has a substantial historical precedent. State interference has been both protective toward and damaging to women, as the state can offer assistance to women in violent situations and also allow conditions to exist that increase women's vulnerability (Dahlerup 1992, 107–108).

Exploring the ideology surrounding the public/private split further reveals the significant relationship between the state and the family. The family as a social unit is not only socially constructed, but historically variable. The changing nature of the family over time points to its inherently political nature. As a result, the organization of the family, including the place of women and the legitimacy of children, becomes a key concern of the political order. The state regulates the lives of women in various ways, including marriage law, abortion law, and welfare (Eisenstein 1983, 53). Historically, these incursions by the state into the private realm have often reinforced women's dependency and secondary standing.

For feminists to challenge domestic violence, they must also challenge the ideology surrounding the public/private split. If the state unavoidably intervenes in the family, then a vital task for feminists is to call for intervention on women's behalf. Yet the historical record serves as a warning; past and current abuses of state power within the private sphere provide compelling grounds for skepticism. This suggests that a theoretical analysis that goes beyond liberalism may be necessary.

There are two points that are particularly important in relation to domestic violence. First, feminist theorists and activists have shown the public/private split to be an ideological camouflage for the state's actual interventions into the private realm. Secondly, because of the political character of family arrangements, the state holds a vital interest in the family itself. These indicate that feminists confronting domestic violence will necessarily encounter the state in the process and that the state is not a neutral player.

Marxism and Feminism

Unlike liberalism, Marxism has a highly developed theory of the state. The theoretical contributions to state theory, while extensive, are not unitary. Marx himself provided more than one explanation of the state, and Marxist theorists have continued to develop conceptions of the state. However, it is possible to establish a few basic Marxist positions concerning the state.

Marxist state theory grapples with the relation among capital, competing classes, and political and economic power. Most commonly, Marxists perceive the state as an instrument of class rule. The function of the state therefore becomes the regulation of conflict among antagonistic classes, which serves to moderate class conflict while continuing the domination of the ruling class and ensuring the continuation of the dominant mode of production. Related to this is a Marxist conception of the state as a system of political domination that affects class struggle. The idea of the state being heavily implicated in the domination of the ruling class raises structural issues concerning the state, a theoretical principle lacking in liberalism (Jessop 1990, 25–29).

Because Marxist theory explains the specific mechanisms by which the state reproduces class inequality, early feminist theorists looked to Marxism as a source of insights into gender. Adopting and modifying various tenets of Marxist theory, these attempts met with varying degrees of success; in fact, Marxist and socialist feminists developed a number of sophisticated accounts (see Barrett 1980; Burstyn 1983; Hartmann 1981; and McIntosh 1978). Within this particular theoretical framework, the state emerges as protecting the interests of the elite class, or bourgeoisie, in part by erecting gender structures that support the capitalist system. The nuclear family exists for the benefit of the state and capital; the subordination of women within the family not only provides domestic labor for individual men but also maintains a reserve work force. Consequently, the modern oppression of women can be seen as a product of the capitalist system (Franzway, Court, and Connell 1989, 19–20).

Despite the theoretical opportunities that exist in efforts to use Marxism to explain the subordination of women, in this context it is more important to consider the possible practical benefits from this approach, as with liberalism. Unlike the liberal state, Marxists argue that the class state is not neutral. That class interests define the state suggests that reform is more difficult than it appears in the liberal paradigm; this can serve as a warning to feminist activists. Furthermore, if the state is structurally implicated in the subordination of women, it becomes possible that the state is more directly involved with domestic violence. If the interests of the capitalist system are also involved, then feminists working to reduce and, ultimately, end domestic violence must confront extremely powerful forces.

In addition, the Marxist focus on class yields insight into the complex and contradictory nature of the state. Unlike liberal feminism, capitalism emerges as a significant factor that contributes to current conditions. As a result, the state can be seen as holding simultaneous commitments to patriarchy, racism, and capitalism. The state's mediation of these conflicting allegiances can produce contradictory results (Eisenstein 1984, 89). For example, employment for women outside the home provides additional labor while also reducing women's economic dependence upon men.

The liberal framework and the Marxist framework thus elicit two different responses from feminist activists. Liberal feminism encourages engagement with the state and provides the hope of achieving reforms that will offer solutions to domestic violence. In contrast, Marxist feminism suggests that the state is deeply implicated in the subordination of women and thus in domestic violence. From this perspective, it would be more useful for feminist activists to pursue avenues outside the state when confronting domestic violence.

The Patriarchal State

In addition to feminist work within liberal and Marxist frameworks, activists and theorists have developed a body of work that focuses specifically upon women, the state, and the state's relation to gender. Rather than attempting to maneuver existing theoretical systems to accommodate women, this third strand of state theory places women at the center of analysis (see MacKinnon 1989). Consequently, these theories appear potentially useful for activists.

Like definitions of the state, definitions of patriarchy are not only multiple, but also often elusive. Notwithstanding the difficulties, an understanding of patriarchy is necessary in this context. The term "patriarchy" itself is frequently contested, yet continues to be common enough to warrant its use here.

The social system known as patriarchy can be defined as the historically produced institutionalization of men's domination over women (Connell 1994, 142–143). Furthermore, although patriarchy is hierarchical and men of different races, classes, and ethnicities occupy different places within it, men are united in their shared relation of dominance over women within the same social group and dependent on other men to maintain this domination (Hartmann 1981, 14–15).

One of the limitations of the term "patriarchy" is the possibility of falsely universalizing male dominance over women. Because patriarchy is such a broad concept, it can obscure the enormous variations in women's experiences and the ways in which women encounter male dominance. Furthermore, the variations in men's experiences, including race, class, and sexual orientation, are also overlooked. Developing a typology of patriarchies is one way to avoid this problem; some examples include capitalist patriarchy, feudal patriarchy, and welfare state patriarchy (Dahlerup 1992, 95–95).

As seen in the discussions above, the concept of patriarchy has been connected to other state theories with varying degrees of success. In liberal feminism, patriarchy is primarily a problem of personnel within the state and sexist attitudes in society. This perception suggests that reform measures can readily address and correct patriarchy. The position of Marxist feminism is different and conceptualizes a much more complex problem. Because patriarchy is essentially linked to the capitalist system, it is deeply entrenched in both the state and society. As will be seen, feminist theories of the gendered state also give patriarchy a central position.

Early second-wave feminist analyses of the state were predominantly Marxist. However, other feminists began casting the state in starkly hostile terms, arguing that the state was irretrievably male-dominated and oppressive to women. From such a perspective, the desire of women to be free is incompatible with establishing client relations with the state. For example, one could argue that a woman who leaves an abusive man and then uses welfare to support herself is simply exchanging one oppressor for another (Presley and Kinsky 1982, 77–78).

Other feminists went to further extremes, claiming that the state and individual men worked together in their use of sexual violence to terrorize women into submission. The state's failure to provide basic bodily protection forces women to make arrangements with individual men to gain protection from other men. Because the state itself is an organization of men, the result is analogous to a male protection racket. The lack of physical protection also suggests that women are not members of political society (Peterson 1977, 360–369).

Such theories cast the state as the direct patriarchal oppressor of women. Not only do men control the state, they use it as an instrument of domination over women. Domestic violence thus emerges as a ploy by the state to subordinate women; the state colludes in leaving women vulnerable to violence, thereby forcing women to be dependent upon individual men. Women cannot turn to the state to seek relief from violence, because the state is directly implicated in that violence.

Although compelling in some ways, such a theoretical position is overly simplistic. Within the patriarchal state model, all men and all women possess the same relationship to the state. Furthermore, this model ignores the complexities of state actions, the capacity of the state to adopt certain reforms that can benefit women, and race and class differences among women and men. Although perceiving the state as the enemy can provide a useful warning for feminists, ultimately such a theory cannot fully explain women's complex relations with the state.

The Gendered State

The inability of both traditional state theories and patriarchal state theory to satisfactorily produce a specifically feminist account of the state has compelled feminist theorists to develop a still emerging model that can be called the "gendered state" model. This model utilizes insights from other state theories, and also engages the mutually constitutive systems of sexism, racism, and classism. As a result, the gendered state model reflects the incoherency and complexity of the state itself.

The liberal, Marxist, and patriarchal state modes each contribute to the gendered state model. Although the gendered state model rejects the assumption of state neutrality, it takes from liberalism the idea of *state accessibility*. The need of the state to at least appear democratic provides an opening for reform efforts. In addition, the rise of the liberal state provides the opportunity for demands for equality; the state must balance its use of power with a search for legitimation. Feminism can thus place demands upon the state which are difficult to evade without risking legitimacy (Connell 1994, 161). Marxism lends the perception that the state is *structurally implicated* in social inequality and the reproduction of social relations. The patriarchal state offers the warning that the state is *masculinist* and deeply influenced by and invested in current gender relations.

The gendered state model, however, does not lend coherency to the state that it does not actually possess. Rather than assuming unitary relations and interests between and among men, women, and capital, this developing model casts the state as erratic and disconnected. The relationship between gender inequalities and the state is fluid; the state both reflects the gender order and constitutes gender relations through its practices. Simultaneously, these gender relations become institutionalized in historically specific state forms. In addition, the gendered state model shifts the focus from a perception of fixed or coherent state structures to an emphasis upon practice and discourse (Pringle and Watson 1992 63–64; see Watson 1990 and Sassoon 1992). Unlike the patriarchal state, the emerging gendered state model perceives the masculinist nature of the state as emanating from the practices, or procedures, of the state. The state's patterns of functioning, the character and dynamics of the state apparatus, and the state's involvement in gender politics as played out in the social arena all hold gendered aspects and need further analysis (Connell 1994, 146).

One consequence is the embedding of certain structures and assumptions about gender into law and policy. Such assumptions include the primacy of heterosexuality as the norm, the economic dependence of women upon men, and the desirability of maintaining the traditional nuclear family. Another example is the "family ethic," the changing social norm that defines women's proper role and has had particular influence upon the development of the welfare state (Abramovitz 1988, 3).

These gendered assumptions, and the state's commitment to the current gender order, structurally constrain the state and limit its actions; as a result, the state is unlikely to create laws or policies that transcend or fundamentally challenge existing gender relations. This is not a reason for feminists to abandon the state, however. Because the gendered state model recognizes the incoherency of the state, it remains aware that the state is a significant player in gender politics. Feminists seeking to change gender relations in society cannot ignore government power.

Since the nineteenth century, the modern liberal state has increasingly assumed responsibilities that previously had been met within the family. The expansion of the public sector, and the state's growing involvement in socialization, education, and the care of the sick and the aged has both diminished the private status of the family and contributed to the state's involvement in public control, intervention, and support (Hernes 1992, 73). Consequently, the liberal state demonstrates a broad involvement in gender relations, including family policy, population policy, labor force and labor market management, regulation of sexual behavior and expression, provision of child care, mass education, taxation and income redistribution, the management of the military, and so on. Gender politics is arguably a major realm of state policy, therefore making the state unavoidable for feminism (Connell 1994, 159).

Although the state is a significant participant in gender politics, it is only part of a wider structure of gender relationships. In other words, the state is a node within the larger network of power relations that constitute the gender order (Connell 1994, 148). The family is another part of this network. The work of French theorist Michel Foucault has influenced the changing perspective of the gendered state model; his conceptualization of power as relational, finding shifting and unstable expression in networks and alliances, casts the state as an effect of these relations. By not assuming that the state acts coherently on behalf of certain privileged groups, Foucault shifts the emphasis from the intentionality of the state to questions concerning the state's techniques and apparatuses of regulation (Pringle and Watson 1992, 55–56).

Foucault characterizes modern power as capillary; in other words, power resides in and touches people through the social practices that constitute everyday life in modern societies (Fraser 1989, 18). From this perspective, domestic violence is a manifestation of the power dynamics in social and intimate relationships. The consequences include the identification of battering as political as well as implicated in the subordination of women.

Because the gendered state model considers the state an active participant in gender relations, the ideas of Foucault present compelling insights. The expression of state power emerges as frequently subtle; the modern state does not simply rely upon overt demonstrations of force to maintain social order. In addition, the recognition of power within social practices suggests that not only are daily actions political, but that there are multiple sites of potential resistance. While the state is significant, it is not the only possible avenue for social change. Feminists must also consider other options.

The emphasis within the gendered state model upon the practices of the state, rather than the coherency or intentions of the state, also leads to an examination of state power. Wendy Brown argues that state power is both historically produced and gendered in specifically masculinist ways. She defines four modalities of state power: the juridical-legislative, or liberal dimension, which includes the formal constitutional aspects of the state; the capitalist dimension, which incorporates both private property rights and the state's involvement in capitalist production, distribution, and consumption; the prerogative dimension, or legitimate arbitrary power, such as that of the military and the police; and the bureaucratic dimension, including the hierarchy and procedures of institutional arrangements. These different forms of power are masculinist in that they both privilege and construct masculinity, albeit in varying ways (Brown 1992, 12–14).

Brown's classification suggests that neither the state nor state power is unitary. Consequently, different branches and departments of the state apparatus exercise varying forms of power. The recognition of this not only further complicates the emerging gendered state model, but also encourages the development of feminist strategy that responds to these differences. Previous chapters in this book provide examples of these different strategies.

The perception of the state as a significant, but not solitary, participant in gender politics suggests that feminist strategy should include engaging the state while simultaneously pursuing other avenues of social change. The emerging gendered state model, borrowing from liberalism, also indicates that the state is responsive to social demands; consequently, the organization of broadly-based mass movements is one way to confront the state and effectively demand reforms. The state, therefore, can be considered a necessary, but not sufficient, arena within which feminists must struggle for social change.

Within the gendered state model, neither the state nor gender is coherent. The current gender order differentiates between men and women while privileging men, while racism differentiates among races while privileging whiteness. These processes, although distinct, are intertwined; gender is racialized and race is gendered. Furthermore, economic class is deeply embedded in the manifestations of gender and race (Eisenstein 1994, 2–3). The experiences of women, for example, are profoundly influenced by race and class.

As a result, the gendered state model, as discussed previously, does not assume unitary relations between and among men and women of varying racial identity and economic class. In terms of strategy, the recognition of these differences becomes absolutely necessary. The effects of laws and policies, including those sought by feminists, can vary significantly for women in diverse contexts. Not all women, nor all men hold the same relationship to the state.

The struggle for laws and policies by feminists and other groups also contributes to the contradictory aspects of the state. Social policy emerges not only from the fragmented and inconsistent goals of policy-makers, but also from the awkwardly constructed compromises that characterize political and social conflict (Gordon 1990a, 23). Feminists may hold clear policy objectives, yet be confronted with the necessity of accepting compromises and changes in order to obtain even limited success. The evolution of the Violence Against Women Act provides an excellent example of this process.

The paradoxical and incoherent nature of the gendered state does create opportunities for feminist strategy, however. The state is vulnerable to pressures from feminist activists because it must ideologically defend itself as a democratic institution; as a result, women have won concessions from the state. Because the state must assure stability in times of social crisis, feminists can create public disturbances in an effort to influence state action. Within this theoretical model, the state emerges as a site of social conflict which is not neutral, yet not impenetrable. As a result, the state can be a paradoxical source of power for women.

Endnotes

Chapter 1

[1] Such as the jurist Gratian (circa 1140), Friar Cherubino (circa 1450), and Martin Luther (1483-1546). The term "wife beating" will be used in this chapter to reflect the language that was used to describe domestic violence against women for most of modern history. "Wife beating" was used until the 1980s in literature, legislation, and scholarship. Clearly this term renders non-married relations of men, such as girlfriends, ex-wives, and live-in partners invisible. The term "wife" poorly reflects the real-life situations of many women. Feminist legal scholars Sue Eisenberg and Patricia Micklow criticize the term "beating" as well. They suggest the term "wife assault" is more accurate than "wife beating," but even "wife assault" is still not legally precise (Eisenberg and Micklow 1977, 140). As will be pointed out in Chapter 2, the language used in domestic violence discourse is critical to understanding the historical moments during which the problem has surfaced in the public arena.

[2] The New English Bible, New York: Cambridge University Press (1961). The passage appears exactly the same in The Holy Bible, New International Version.

[3] These agencies are considered part of the state. While they were not operated directly by the government at first, they performed functions we consider to be governmental functions today and had a clear interest in regulating behavior and maintaining social "order." See the Appendix for our definition of "the state."

[4] Also, see in this chapter, the discussion of the battered women's movement and how a similar split emerged between radical feminist shelter organizers and mainstream social service personnel.

[5] Women comprised less than 3% of the House of Representatives in 1945-47, and 0% of the Senate (Center for the American Woman and politics, 1996).

Chapter 2

[1] See Ann Jones (1994, 104) for the case of Patricia Washington and other women sentenced to prison terms much longer than those given to men who kill their spouses, girlfriends, or ex's.

[2] Deborah Rhode (1989) states that while men and children, especially girls, are victims of domestic abuse, it is important to focus explicitly on the abuse women face in family relations that are reinforced in a culture of gender inequality (237). Also, as Ann Jones (1994) notes, domestic violence is a seemingly innocuous term for an incredibly violent phenomena perpetuated by men against women. The disadvantage of relying on "domestic violence" as a term is that it sugar-coats the issue so to speak, by making it more palatable, less explicit, and less politically radical.

[3] Sharon Marcus (1992, 388) makes this point in relation to rape, where she argues feminists should advocate preventive rape measures which "will empower women to take the ability to rape completely out of men's hands." See also Ann Jones, 1994.

[4] Some recent books that use "family violence" as the category in which to include wife or woman abuse are Ohlin and Tonry (1989) and Walker (1990).

[5] The criminal code deals with assault and battery and is a crime against the state which is enforced by the state (Kampmann, 1989: 106). The civil code encompasses violations of individual freedom and civil rights which would allow women to sue their attackers by seeking "compensatory and punitive damages through federal courts for a crime of violence motivated—at least in part—by animus toward the victim's gender" (Hirshman 1994, 46, offers a good overview of this shift in legal prosecution).

[6] See also Bograd (1988) and Schechter (1982) for critiques of the gender neutrality of family violence and domestic violence.

[7] For recent studies of abuse in gay and lesbian relationships see Island and Latellier (1991), Lobel (1986).

[8] See Copelon (1994, 291-367) for a thought-provoking argument to address domestic violence through international laws against torture. There is a variety of scholarship on women's rights as human rights available. See for example, Bunch (1995).

[9] There are cautions to be raised when relying on rights. Wendy Brown (1995) offers a critical and important feminist analysis of the double-edged sword of rights which while offering potentially progressive actions also reinscribe injured identities which may do more to regulate than to free particular, marginalized identities.

[10] The debate around liberal rights as property rights has been especially problematic for women and slaves, who were historically were considered property themselves and therefore without rights. The basis of liberal rights in the concept of private property has recently been addressed by Rosalind Pollack Petchesky (1995). See also Daniels (1993) and Petchesky (1990) who utilize the notion of bodily integrity to defend a woman's right to reproductive freedom and abortion.

[11] Yet even such a proto-feminist theorist such as J.S. Mill made distinctions among women; in particular in relation to class. This class distinction may serve to undermine his arguments for female equality, or reveal even deeper cracks in liberal theory in terms of the relationship between gender and class. See Zerilli (1994) for an insightful analysis of this issue.

[12] The sameness versus difference debate in feminist theory and practice has generated much scholarship and controversy. See Scott (1988) and Jones (1990) for a good review of these issues.

Chapter 3

[1] 595 F. Supp. 1521 (Dist. Conn. 1984)

[2] See Ann Jones (1994) pp. 153-161 for a discussion of how the interests of the male research establishment were served by this funding decision.

[3] This sketch is drawn from the author's experience as a crime victim's advocate.

[4] It is reasonable that a woman may want her abusive partner to receive treatment whether or not she plans to reconcile. Treatment programs for batterers are discussed further in Chapter Four. Susan Schechter (see Chapter One) has spoken about leaving an abusive partner as a process that, for some women, involves coming to grips with the fact that he is not going to change. The process may also require women to learn by trial and error what steps are necessary to truly get away or insure safety -- in some cases extreme steps such as completely severing ties with family and friends(through whom women can be traced) or leaving the country are necessary.

[5] Based on reports from three states that are closely monitoring arrests of women in cases of domestic violence between heterosexual partners, Joan Zorza (National Battered Women's Law Project of the National Center Women and Family Law) estimates that 95% of the women participating in mandatory batterer treatment programs are there as a result of actions taken in self-defense or because they have been wrongfully accused. Personal communication, April, 1995.

[6] Based on information received from feminists monitoring this situation in various states, Joan Zorza (National Battered Women's Law Project of the National Center on Women and Family Law) estimates that batterers receive sole custody or shared custody rights in 70% of the cases in which they sue for child custody. Personal communication, April, 1995. According to Saunders (1994), men who batter are likely to remarry sooner and have higher incomes than their ex-partners, factors that give them an edge in custody battles.

[7] Feminists' success in educating the public about domestic violence and gaining support for battered women's programs is undoubtedly related to greater public recognition of and support for many types of victims. For example, in the last decade, the campaign organized by families of drunk driving victims has effectively changed both the social norms and the legal penalties regarding driving while under the influence of alcohol.

[8] Pat Eng of the Asian Women's Center in New York City finds that many immigrant battered women do not want to involve the police. However, they may be faced with police involvement when someone else, usually a family member or neighbor, intervenes. Personal communication, June, 1995.

Chapter 4

[1] The "pie-chart model" described here is taken from a flier published by the Domestic Abuse Intervention Project, 206 West Fourth Street, Duluth, Minnesota, 55806; (218) 722-4134.

Chapter 5

[1] The author gratefully acknowledges the invaluable information provided by NOW Legal Defense and Education Fund, particularly Pat Reuss and Nicole Brown in the Washington, D.C. office and Kathleen Lyons in the New York City office.

[2] See also Costain and Costain (1987), for a discussion of women's interest groups and political parties and Walker (1991), for a theoretical discussion of the process by which interest groups emerge, gain influence, and function in the U.S. context.

[3] In 1990 Congress also passed a resolution on domestic violence which created a presumption that it is detrimental for a child to be placed in the custody of an abusive parent. While this resolution does not have legislative status, it was passed in hopes of encouraging states to make such laws. The Immigration Act of 1990 included a provision which permitted foreigners in abusive marriages to American citizens to leave their spouses without risk of deportation. These measures were the only federal initiatives which addressed the problem of domestic violence against women. In light of this situation, the magnitude and importance of the Violence Against Women Act is easily argued.

[4] For tracking of the legislation in and out of committee and for specifics on floor votes see *Congressional Quarterly Weekly Reports.* Memoranda, minutes from meetings, and fact sheets from NOW LDEF were also used in following changes in the provisions of VAWA, especially during its progress in 1994.

[5] Statistics compiled by the Congressional Caucus for Women's Issues.

Chapter 6

[1] Senator Joseph Biden, *Violence Against Women: Victims of the System*, U.S. Senate Committee on the Judiciary, 101st Congress, 2d Session, Senate Hearing 102-369 (April 9, 1991). Cited in *Issues Quarterly: An Intelligent Resource for Research, Policy and Action Affecting the Lives of Women and Girls*. 1:2, p. 10.

[2] For a discussion of how heterosexist norms are enforced by the labeling of some women as "man-hating lesbians," see Pharr (1993). In prevailing gender ideology, the negative term "man-hating" is applied to women who reject dependency on men, but the term "women-hating," which could apply to men who sexually harass women, to batterers, rapists, and consumers of violent pornography, does not have comparable pejorative weight and is rarely used.

[3] See Matthews (1994) for a discussion of the related phenomenon of bureaucratization as it occurred in rape crisis programs. According to Matthews, in the bureaucratic process, maintenance of the organization becomes more important than the organization's original purpose.

[4] This act includes spouses and cohabitants in its definition of domestic violence, and has special provisions for the abuse of the elderly and disabled, as well as women and children.

[5] Prevention of Domestic Violence Act of 1991. L.1991, c. 261, 1, eff. Nov. 12, 1991.

Bibliography

Abramovitz, Mimi. 1988. *Regulating the lives of women: Social welfare policy from colonial times to the present.* Boston: South End Press.

Ackelsberg, Martha A. 1988. Communities, resistance, and women's activism: Some implications for a democratic polity. In *Women and the politics of empowerment,* edited by A. Bookman and S. Morgan. Philadelphia: Temple University Press.

Adams, David. 1989. Stages of anti-sexist awareness and change for men who batter. In *Family violence: Emerging issues of a national crisis,* edited by L. J. Dickstein and C. C. Nadelson. Washington, D.C.: American Psychiatric Press.

Ahrens, Lois. 1980. Battered women's refuges: Feminist cooperatives or social service institutions? *Aegis: Magazine on Ending Violence Against Women*, summer, 9–15.

Bachman, Ronet. 1994. *Violence against women: A national crime victimization survey report.* U.S. Department of Justice.

Baltimore Sun. 1994. 'Us kind of ladies' didn't get hit. July 3.

Bako, Yolanda. 1980. Questions for the battered women's movement. *Aegis: Magazine for Ending Violence Against Women.* Summer/Autumn, 5-8.

Barbee, Evelyn L. 1992. Ethnicity and woman abuse in the United States. In *Violence against women: Nursing research, education, and practice issues,* edited by C. M. Sampselle. New York: Hemisphere Publishing Corporation.

Barrett, Michele. 1980. *Women's oppression today: Problems in Marxist feminist analysis.* London: Verso.

Bart, Pauline and Eileen Geil Moran, eds. 1993. *Violence against women: The bloody footprints.* Newbury Park, CA: Sage Publications.

Belluck, Pam. 1997. Women's killers very often husbands or boyfriends, study finds. *New York Times*, March 31: B2.

Besharov, Douglas J. 1990. *Family violence: Research and public policy issues.* Washington, D.C.: The AEI Press.

Bograd, Michele. 1988. Feminist perspectives on wife abuse: An introduction. In *Feminist perspectives on wife* abuse, edited by K. Yllö and M. Bograd. Newbury Park: Sage Publications.

Bookman, Ann, and Sandra Morgan, eds. 1988. *Women and the politics of empowerment.* Philadelphia: Temple University Press.

Boneparth, Ellen and Emily Stoper, eds. 1988. *Women, power and policy: Toward the year 2000.* 2nd edition. New York: Pergamon Press.

Bourg, Sherrie and Harley V. Stock. 1994. A review of domestic violence arrest statistics in a police department using a pro-arrest policy: Are pro-arrest policies enough? *Journal of Family Violence* 9 (2): 177–189.

Bowman, Cynthia. 1992. The arrest experiments: A feminist critique. *The Journal of Law & Criminology* 83 (1): 201–208.

Brown, Wendy. 1992. Finding the man in the state. *Feminist Studies* 18 (1): 7–34.

Brown, Wendy. 1995. *States of injury: Power and freedom in late modernity.* Princeton: Princeton University Press.

Buchwald, Claire. 1993. Training for safehouse. In *Transforming a rape culture,* edited by E. Buchwald, P. Fletcher and M. Roth. Minneapolis: Milkweed Editions.

Buchwald, Emilie, Panela Fletcher and Martha Roth, eds. 1993. *Transforming a rape culture*. Minneapolis: Milkweed Editions.

Bunch, Charlotte. 1979. The reform tool kit. *Aegis: Magazine on Ending Violence Against Women,* July/August: 25–34.

Bunch, Charlotte. 1995. Transforming human rights from a feminist perspective. In *Women's rights, human rights: International feminist perspectives*, edited by J. S. Peters and A. Wolper. New York: Routledge.

Burstyn, Varda. 1983. Masculine dominance and the state. In *The Socialist register 1983,* edited by R. Miliband and J. Saville. London: The Merlin Press.

Butler, Judith, Joan Scott, eds. 1992. *Feminists Theorize the Political.* New York: Routledge.

Buzawa, Eve, and Carl Buzawa. 1993a. The impact of arrest on domestic violence: introduction. *American Behavioral Scientist* 36 (5): 558–574.

———. 1993b. The scientific evidence is not conclusive: Arrest is no panacea. In *Current controversies on family violence,* edited by R. Gelles and D. Loseke. Newbury Park, CA: Sage.

Cagan, Leslie. 1992. Community organizing and the religious right: Lessons from the Measure 9 campaign (an interview with Suzanne Pharr). *Radical America*, 24 (4): 67-75.

Carroll, Susan J. 1995. A mixed verdict: The impact of women on the crime bill. Paper delivered at the annual meeting of the Midwest Political Science Association, Chicago, IL.

Carroll, Susan J., Debra L. Dodson, and Ruth B. Mandel. 1991. *The impact of women in public office.* New Brunswick, NJ: Center for the American Woman and Politics.

Center for the American Woman and Politics. 1996. *Winter Fact Sheet.* New Brunswick, NJ: Center for the American Woman and Politics.

Center for Women Policy Studies. 1991. *Violence against women as bias motivated hate crime: Defining the issues.* Washington, D.C.: Center for Women Policy Studies.

Chambliss, William. 1995. Crime control and ethnic minorities: Legitimizing racial oppression by creating moral panics. In *Ethnicity, race, and crime: Perspectives across time and place*, edited by D. Hawkins. Albany, NY: State University of New York Press.

Clear, Todd. 1996. Panel on crime/criminal justice. *Racism, and public policy conference*, Rutgers University (Bloustein School of Planning and Public Policy). New Brunswick, NJ.

Cohen, Sherrill. 1992. *The evolution of women's asylums since 1500: From refuges for ex-prostitutes to shelters for battered women.* New York: Oxford University Press.

Congressional Caucus for Women's Issues. 1993. Violence against women act reintroduced; Targeted as top priority. *Update: Newsletter of Congressional Caucus for Women's Issues,* 26 February.

Connell, Robert W. 1994. The state, gender, and sexual politics: Theory and appraisal. In *Power/gender: Social relations in theory and practice,* edited by H. L. Radtke and H. J. Stam. London: Sage Publications.

Cook, Elizabeth Adell, Sue Thomas, and Clyde Wilcox, eds. 1994. *The year of the woman: Myths and realities.* Boulder, CO: Westview Press, Inc.

Copelon, Rhonda. 1994. Recognizing the egregious in the everyday: Domestic violence as torture. *Columbia Human Rights Law Review*: 25 (2): 291-367.

Costain, Anne N. 1988. Representing women: The transition from social movement to interest group. In *Women, power and policy: Toward the year 2000,* 2nd ed., edited by E. Boneparth and E. Stoper. New York: Pergamon Press.

Costain, Anne N., and W. Douglass Costain. 1987. Strategy and tactics of the women's movement in the United States: The role of political parties. In *The women's movements of the United States and Western Europe: Consciousness, political opportunity, and public policy,* edited by M. Katzenstein and C. Mueller. Philadelphia: Temple University Press.

Crenshaw, Kimberle. 1992. Whose story is it anyhow? Feminist and antiracist appropriations of Anita Hill. In *Race-ing Justice, en-gendering power: Essays on Anita Hill, Clarence Thomas, and the construction of social reality,* edited by T. Morrison. New York: Pantheon Books.

D.C. Area Feminist Alliance Task Force on Violence Against Women. 1979. March to stop violence against women—underlying principles. *Aegis: Magazine on Ending Violence Against Women,*May/June: 37–41.

Dahlerup, Drude. 1992. Confusing concepts—confusing reality: A theoretical discussion of the patriarchal state. In *Women and the state: The shifting bounds of public and private,* edited by A. S. Sassoon. New York: Routledge.

Daniels, Cynthia R. 1993. *At women's expense: State power and the politics of fetal rights.* Cambridge: Harvard University Press.

Davidson, Terry. 1978. *Conjugal crime: Understanding and changing the wifebeating pattern.* New York: Hawthorn Books.

Davis, Liane, Jan Hagen, and Theresa Early. 1994. Social services for battered women: Are they adequate, accessible, and appropriate? *Social Work: Journal of the National Association of Social Workers* 39 (6): 695–704.

Davis, Angela. 1983. *Women, race and class.* New York: Vintage Books.

Declaration of Sentiments and Resolutions, Seneca Falls, 1848. 1990. In *Issues in feminism: An introduction to women's studies*, 2nd edition, edited by Shelia Ruth. Mountain View, CA: Mayfield Publishing Company.

Diamond, Irene, ed. 1983. *Families, politics, and public policy: A feminist dialogue on women and the state.* New York: Longman.

Dickstein, Leah and Carol Nadelson, eds. 1989. *Family violence: Emerging issues of a national crisis.* Washington, D.C.: American Psychiatric Press.

Dobash, R. Emerson and Russell P. Dobash. 1992. *Women, violence, and social change.* New York: Routledge.

Dodson, Debra L. and Susan J. Carroll. 1991. Reshaping the agenda: Women in state legislatures. New Brunswick, NJ: Center for the American Woman and Politics.

DuBois, Ellen Carol. 1978. *Feminism and suffrage: The emergence of an independent women's movement in America, 1848–1869.* Ithaca: Cornell University Press.

Dutton, Mary Ann and Lisa A. Goodman. 1994. Posttraumatic stress disorder among battered women: Analysis of legal implications. *Behavioral Sciences and the Law,* 12 (3): 215–234.

Dworkin, Andrea. 1981. *Pornography: Men Possessing Women.* New York: Putman.

Edwards, Susan. 1989. *Policing "domestic" violence: Women,the law, and the state.* Newbiru Park, CA: Sage Publications.

Eisenberg, Susan, and Patricia Micklow. 1977. The assaulted wife: "Catch-22" revisited. *Women's Rights Law Reporter,* 3: 138–161.

Eisenstein, Zillah R. 1981. *The radical future of liberal feminism.* New York: Longman.

———. 1983. The state, the patriarchal family, and working mothers. In *Families, politics, and public policy,* edited by Irene Diamond. New York: Longman.

———. 1984. *Feminism and sexual equality: Crisis in liberal America.* New York: Monthly Review Press.

———. 1994. *The color of gender: Reimaging democracy.* Berkeley: University of California Press.

Ewing, Charles. 1990. Psychological self-defense: A proposed justification for battered women who kill. *Law and Human Behavior,* 14 (6): 579–594.

Ewing, Charles. 1987. *Battered women who kill: Psychological self-defense as legal justification.* Lexington, MA: Lexington Books.

Faigman, David L. 1986. The battered woman syndrome and self-defense. *Virginia Law Review* 72: 619–647.

Ferraro, Kathleen and Lucille Pope. 1993. Irreconcilable differences: Battered women, police, and the law. In *Legal responses to wife assault: Current trends and evaluation,* edited by N. Z. Hilton. Newbury Park, CA: Sage.

Ferraro, Kathleen J. 1993. Cops, courts and woman battering. In *Violence against women: The bloody footprints,* edited by P. Bart and E. Moran. Newbury Park, CA: Sage Publications.

———. 1989. The legal response to woman battering in the United States. In *Women, policing, and male violence: international perspectives*, edited by J. Hanmer, J. Radford, and E. Stanko. London: Routledge.

Ferree, Myra and Patricia Martin, eds. 1995. *Feminist organizations: Harvest of the new women's movement.* Philadelphia: Temple University Press.

Florida Supreme Court. 1990. 'Where the injured fly for justice': Reforming practices which impede the dispensation of justice to minorities in Florida. Report submitted to the Florida Supreme Court by the Racial and Ethnic Bias Study Commission.

Franzway, Suzanne, Dianne Court, and R.W. Connell. 1989. *Staking a claim: Feminism, bureaucracy, and the state.* Boston: Allen and Unwin.

Fraser, Nancy. 1989. *Unruly practices: Power, discourse, and gender in contemporary social theory.* Minneapolis: University of Minnesota Press.

Freud, Sigmund [1933] 1965. *New introductory lectures on psychoanalysis.* Vol. 2. Translated and edited by James Strachey. Pelican Freud Library: Penguin Books.

Friedman, Deb. 1979. Increased convictions? Or lowered expectations? *Aegis: Magazine on Ending Violence Against Women,* July/August: 15–17.

Gee, Pauline. 1983. Ensuring police protection for battered women: The *Scott v. Hart* suit. *Signs,* 8 (3): 554–567.

Gelles, Richard and Donileen Loseke, eds. 1993. *Current controversies on family violence*. Newbury Park, CA: Sage.

Gerth, Hans H. and C. Wright Mills, eds. 1958. *From Max Weber: Essays in sociology*. New York: Oxford University Press.

Giddings, Paula. 1985. *When and where I enter: The impact of black women on race and sex in America.* New York: Bantam Books.

Gilligan, Carol. 1982. *In a different voice: Psychological theory and women's development.* Cambridge, MA: Harvard University Press.

Ginsberg, Faye and Rayna Rapp, eds. 1995. *Conceiving the New World Order.* Berkeley: University of California.

Gondolf, Edward W. 1993. Treating the batterer. In *Battering and family therapy: A feminist perspective,* edited by M. Hansen and M. Harway. Newbury Park, CA: Sage Publications.

Gordon, Linda. 1989. *Heroes of their own lives: The politics and history of family violence, Boston 1880–1960.* New York: Penguin Books.

———. 1990a. The new feminist scholarship on the welfare state. In *Women, the state, and welfare,* edited by L. Gordon. Madison: University of Wisconsin Press.

———. 1990b. Family violence, feminism, and social control. In *Women, the state, and welfare,* edited by Linda Gordon. Madison: University of Wisconsin Press.

Greenwald, Jessica P., Alan J. Tomkins, Mary Kenning, and Denis Zavodny. 1990. Psychological self-defense jury instructions: Influence on verdicts for battered women defendants. *Behavioral Sciences and the Law,* 8(2): 171–180.

Hagan, John and Ruth Peterson, eds. 1995. *Crime and inequality*. Stanford, CA: Stanford University Press.

Hamberger, L. Kevin and James E. Hastings. 1993. Court-mandated treatment of men who assault their partners. In *Legal responses to wife assault: Current trends and evaluation,* edited by N. Z. Hilton. Newbury Park, CA: Sage Publications.

Hanmer, Jalna, Jill Radford and Elizabeth Stanko, eds. 1989. *Women, policing, and male violence: international perspectives*. London: Routledge.

Hansen, Marsali and Michele Harway, eds. 1993. *Battering and family therapy: A feminist perspective*. Newbury Park: Sage Publications.

Hart, Barbara. 1993. Battered women and the criminal justice system. *American Behavioral Scientist,* 36 (5): 624–638.

Hartmann, Heidi. 1981. The unhappy marriage of Marxism and feminism: Towards a more progressive union. In *Women and revolution,* edited by L. Sargent. Boston: South End Press.

Hawkins, Darnell F., ed. 1995. *Ethnicity, race, and crime: Perspectives across time and place*. Albany, NY: State University of New York Press.

Herman, Judith. 1992. *Trauma and recovery*. New York: Basic Books.

Hernes, Maria Helga. 1992. Women and the welfare state: The transition from public to private dependence. In *Women and the State: The Shifting Boundaries of Public and Private,* edited by A. S. Sassoon. New York: Routledge.

Hilton, N. Zoe, ed. 1993. *Legal responses to wife assault: current trends and evaluation*. Newbury Park, CA: Sage.

Hirshman, Linda. 1994. Making safety a civil right. *Ms.,* 2 (September/October): 44–47.

Idelson, Holly. 1994a. More cops, jails: House takes a $28 billion aim at crime. *Congressional Quarterly Weekly Report,* 23 April: 1001–1004.

———. 1994b. Racial sentencing provision snarls crime legislation. *Congressional Quarterly Weekly Report,* 25 June: 1713.

———. 1994c. $33 billion crime measure heads to last hurdles. *Congressional Quarterly Weekly Report,* 25 June: 2137–2140.

——— and Richard Sammon. 1994. Marathon talks produce new anti-crime bill. *Congressional Quarterly Weekly Report,* 20 August: 2249–2254.

Island, David and Patrick Letellier. 1991. *Men who beat the men who love them: Battered gay men and domestic violence.* New York: Haworth Press.

Jaffe, P., E. Hastings, D. Reitzel, and G. Austin. 1993. The impact of police laying charges in legal responses to wife assault: Current trends and evaluation. In *Legal responses to wife assault: current trends and evaluation,* edited by N. Z. Hilton. Newbury Park, CA: Sage.

Jessop, Robert. 1990. *State theory: Putting the Capitalist state in its place.* University Park: Pennsylvania State University Press.

Jones, Ann. 1994. *Next time, she'll be dead: Battering and how to stop it.* Boston: Beacon Press.

Jones, Kathleen B. 1990. Citizenship in a woman-friendly polity. *Signs* 15 (4): 781–812.

Kampmann, Maryanne E. 1993. The legal victimization of battered women. *Women's Rights Law Reporter* 15 (1): 101–113.

Kasian, Marilyn, Nicholas P. Spanos, Cheryl A. Terrance, and Suzanne Peebles. 1993. Battered women who kill: Jury simulation and legal defenses. *Law and Human Behavior* 17(3): 289–312.

Katzenstein, Mary Fainsod and Carol McClurg Mueller. 1987. *The women's movements of the United States and Western Europe: Consciousness, political opportunity, and public policy.* Philadelphia: Temple University Press.

Kraditor, Aileen. 1981. *The ideas of the woman suffrage movement, 1890–1920.* New York: Norton.

Kuhn, Annette and AnneMarie Wolpe, eds. 1978. *Feminism and materialism: Women and modes of production.* London: Routledge and Kegan Paul.

Lerman, Lisa. 1992. The decontextualization of domestic violence. *The Journal of Criminal Law & Criminology,* 83 (1): 217–240.

Littleton, Christine. 1989. Women's experience and the problem of transition: Perspectives on male battering of women. *The University of Chicago Legal Forum,* 1989: 23-57.

Lobel, Kerry, ed. 1986. *Naming the violence: Speaking out about lesbian battering.* Seattle: Seal Press.

Loewenberg, Bert and Ruth Bogin. 1976. *Black women in nineteenth-century American life: Their words, their thoughts, their feelings.* University Park, PA: The Pennsylvania State University Press.

MacKinnon, Catharine A. 1989. *Toward a feminist theory of the state.* Cambridge: Harvard University Press.

Mahoney, Martha R. 1991. Legal images of battered women: Redefining the issue of separation. *Michigan Law Review*, 90 (1): 35–75.

Marcus, Sharon. 1992. Fighting bodies, fighting words: A theory and politics of rape prevention. In *Feminists Theorize the Political*, edited by J. Butler and J. W. Scott. New York: Routledge.

Martin, Patricia and Robert Hummer. 1993. Fraternities and rape on campus. In *Violence against women: The bloody footprints,* edited by P. Bart and E. Moran. Newbury Park, CA: Sage.

Martinez, Marion. 1979. Cultural diversity in shelters. *Aegis: Magazine on Ending Violence Against Women*, March/April, 40–41.

Maryland Special Joint Committee on Gender Bias in the Courts. 1989. Domestic violence and the courts. *RESPONSE* 12: 3–6.

Matthews, Nancy. 1994. *Confronting rape: The feminist anti-rape movement and the state*. New York: Routledge.

McIntosh, Mary. 1978. The state and the oppression of women. In *Feminism and materialism: Women and modes of production,* edited by A. Kuhn and A. Wolpe. London: Routledge and Kegan Paul.

Mezey, Susan Gluck. 1994. Increasing the number of women in office: Does it matter? In *The year of the woman,* edited by E.A. Cook, S. Thomas, and C. Wilcox. Boulder, CO: Westview Press, Inc.

Miliband, R., and J. Saville. 1983. *The Socialist register 1983*. London: The Merlin Press.

Mill, John Stuart. 1991. *On Liberty and other essays*, edited with an introduction by John Gray. Oxford: Oxford University Press.

Moi, Toril. 1985. *Sexual/textual politics: Feminist literary theory*. New York: Methuen.

Moore, Donna M., ed. 1979. *Battered women.* Beverly Hills: Sage Publications.

Morgan, Robin, ed. 1970. *Sisterhood is powerful: An anthology of writings from the women's liberation movement.* New York: Vintage Books.

Morrison, Toni. 1992. *Race-ing Justice, en-gendering power: Essays on Anita Hill, Clarence Thomas, and the construction of social reality.* New York: Pantheon Books.

Morse, Stephen J. 1990. The misbegotten marriage of soft psychology and bad law: Psychological self-defense as a justification for homicide. *Law and Human Behavior,* 14 (6): 595–618.

New Jersey Coalition for Battered Women. 1994. *Coalition Reporter.* Winter issue. Trenton, NJ: New Jersey Coalition for Battered Women.

New Jersey State Department of Community Affairs. 1994. Division on Women. *Domestic violence: The shameful facts.* Trenton.

New York Times. 1994. She strays, he shoots, judge winks. A:22, October 22.

Ohlin, Lloyd and Michael Tonry, eds. 1989. *Family violence.* Chicago: University of Chicago Press.

Okin, Susan Moller. 1989. *Justice, gender and the family.* New York: Basic Books.

Okun, Lewis. 1986. *Woman abuse: facts replacing myths.* Albany: State University of New York Press.

Oppenlander, Nan. 1981. The evolution of law and wife abuse. *Law and Policy Quarterly,* 3: 382–405.

Osthoff, Sue. 1992. Restoring justice: Clemency for battered women. *RESPONSE,* 14: 2–3.

Pence, Ellen and Melanie Shepard. 1988. Integrating feminist theory and practice: The challenge of the battered women's movement. In *Feminist perspectives on wife abuse*, edited by K. Yllo and M. Bograd. Newbury Park, CA: Sage Publications.

Petchesky, Rosalind Pollack. 1995. The body as property: A feminist re-vision. In *Conceiving the New World Order,* edited by F. Ginsberg and R. Rapp. Berkeley: University of California.

Petchesky, Rosalind Pollack. 1990. *Abortion and women's choice: The state, sexuality, and reproductive freedom.* Boston: Northeastern University Press.

Peters, Julie Stone and Andrea Wolper, eds. 1995. *Women's rights, human rights: International feminist perspectives.* New York: Routledge.

Peterson, Susan Rae. 1977. Coercion and rape: The state as a male protection racket. In *Feminism and Philosophy,* edited by M. Vetterling-Braggin, F. A. Elliston, and J. English. Totowa: Littlefield, Adams, and Co.

Pharr, Suzanne. 1993. Homophobia: A weapon of sexism. In *Feminist frameworks: Alternative theoretical accounts of the relations between women and men*, edited by A. Jaggar and P. Rothenberg. New York: McGraw-Hill.

Pleck, Elizabeth. 1987. *Domestic tyranny: the making of social policy against family violence from colonial times to the present.* New York: Oxford University Press.

Presley, Sharon and Lynn Kinsky. 1982. Government is women's enemy. In *Freedom, feminism, and the state,* edited by W. McElroy. New York: Holmes & Meier.

Pringle, Rosemary and Sophie Watson. 1992. 'Women's interests' and the post-structuralist state. In *Destabilizing theory: Contemporary feminist debates,* edited by M. Barret and A. Phillips. Stanford: Stanford University Press.

Radtke, H. Lorraine, Henderikus J. Stam, eds. 1994. *Power/gender: Social relations in theory and practice.* London: Sage Publications.

Reinelt, Claire. 1995. Moving onto the terrain of the state: The battered women's movement and the politics of engagement. In *Feminist organizations: Harvest of the new women's movement*, edited by M. Ferree and P. Martin. Philadelphia: Temple University Press.

Renzetti, Claire M. 1993. Violence in lesbian relationships. In *Battering and family therapy: A feminist perspective,* edited by M. Hansen and M. Harway. Newbury Park, CA: Sage Publications.

Reuss, Patricia and Sally Goldfarb. 1990-1994. Newsletters, minutes from violence against women task force meetings, and violence against women task force memoranda. National Organization for Women Legal Defense and Education Fund, Washington, D.C., New York, Photocopied.

Rhode, Deborah. 1989. *Justice & gender: Sex discrimination and the law.* Cambridge: Harvard University Press.

Riley, Denise. 1990. *Am I that name? Feminism and the category of 'women' in history.* Minneapolis: University of Minnesota.

Rios, Elsa. 1995. Double jeopardy: Cultural and systemic barriers faced by the latina battered women. Unpublished paper.

Roberts, Albert R. 1981. *Sheltering battered women: A national study and service guide.* New York: Springer Publishing Co.

Roberts, Sam. 1995. Women's work: What's new, what isn't. *The New York Times*, April 27: B6.

Rodriguez, Noelie Maria. 1988. Transcending bureaucracy: feminist politics at a shelter for battered women. *Gender and Society*, 2 (2): 214–227.

Roesch, Ronald, et al. 1993. Legal responses to wife assault: Future prospects for intervention and evaluation. In *Legal Responses to Wife Assault: Current Trends and Evaluation,* edited by N. Z. Hilton. Newbury Park: Sage Publications.

Ruth, Sheila, ed. 1990. *Issues in feminism: An introduction to women's studies*, 2nd edition. Mountain View, CA: Mayfield Publishing Company.

Sampselle, Carolyn M. , ed. 1991. *Violence against women: Nursing research, education, and practice issues.* New York: Hemisphere Publishing Corporation.

Sanday, Peggy. 1990. *Fraternity gang rape: Sex, brotherhood, and privilege on campus.* New York: New York University.

Sargent, Lydia, ed. 1981. *Women and revolution: A discussion of the unhappy marriage of Marxism and feminism.* Boston: South End Press.

Sassoon, Anne Showstack. 1992. Introduction: The personal and the intellectual, fragments and order, international trends and national specificities. In *Women and the state: The shifting boundaries of public and private,* edited by A. S. Sassoon. New York: Routledge.

Saunders, Daniel. 1994. Child custody decisions in families experiencing woman abuse. *Social Work*, 39 (1): 51-59.

Schechter, Susan. 1982. *Women and male violence: the visions and struggles of the battered women's movement.* Boston: South End Press.

———. 1979. Towards an analysis of the persistence of violence against women in the home. *Aegis: Magazine on Ending Violence Against Women*, July/August, 51–52.

Schmidt, Janell and Lawrence Sherman. 1993. Does arrest deter domestic violence? *American Behavioral Scientist*, 36 (5): 601–609.

Schneider, Elizabeth. 1980. Equal rights to trial for women: Sex bias in the law of self-defense. *Harvard Civil Rights-Civil Liberties Law Review,* 15: 631–640.

Schuller, Regina A. and Neil Vidmar. 1992. Battered woman syndrome evidence in the courtroom. *Law and Human Behavior*, 16 (3): 273–291.

Scott, Joan W. 1988. Deconstructing equality-versus-difference: Or, the uses of poststructuralist theory for feminism. *Feminist Studies*, 14 (1): 33–50.

Sears, Vickie. 1992. On the healing road. *The Women's Review of Books*, 9: 10–11.

Seligman, Martin. 1975. *Helplessness: On depression, development and death.* New York: Scribner.

Sheptychi, J. W. 1993. *Innovations in policing domestic violence: Evidence from metropolitan London.* Brookfield, VT: Avebury.

Sherman, Lawrence and Richard Berk. 1984. The specific deterrent effects of arrest for domestic assault. *American Sociological Review,* 49: 261–272.

Skowronek, Stephen. 1982. *Building a new american state: The expansion of national administrative capacities, 1877–1920.* New York: Cambridge University Press.

Spivak, Gayatri Chakravorty. 1987. *In other worlds: Essays in cultural politics.* New York: Methuen.

Stanko, Elizabeth. 1989. Missing the mark? Policing battering. In *Women, policing, and male violence: International perspectives,* edited by J. Hanmer, J. Radford and E. Stanko. London: Routledge.

Stark, Evan. 1993. Mandatory arrest of batterers: A reply to its critics. *American Behavioral Scientist,* 36 (5): 651–680.

Stordeur, Richard A. and Richard Stille, eds. 1989. *Ending men's violence against their partners: One road to peace.* Newbury Park: Sage Publications.

Studer, Marlena. 1984. Wife beating as a social problem: The process of definition. *Women's Studies International Forum,* 7: 412–422.

Thomas, Sue. 1994. *How women legislate.* New York: Oxford University Press.

Tierney, Kate. 1982. The battered women movement and the creation of wife beating problem. *Social Problems,* 29 (3): 207–220.

Tompkins, Alan J. et al. 1993. Self-defense jury instructions in trials of battered women who kill their partner. In *Legal Responses to Wife Assault: Current Trends and Evaluation,* edited by N. Z. Hilton. Newbury Park, CA: Sage Publications.

Vetterling-Braggin, Mary, Frederick Elliston, and Jane English. 1977. *Feminism and Philosophy.* Totowa: Littlefield, Adams, and Co.

Violence Intervention Program. 1995. Mission statement. New York, New York.

Walby, Sylvia. 1990. *Theorizing patriarchy.* Cambridge, Mass.: Basil Blackwell Ltd.

Walker, Gillian. 1990. *Family violence and the women's movmeent: The conceptual politics of struggle.* Toronto: University of Toronto Press.

Walker, Jack L., Jr. 1991. *Mobilizing interest groups in america: Patrons, professions, and social movements.* Ann Arbor, MI: University of Michigan Press.

Walker, Lenore. 1979. *The battered woman.* New York: Harper and Row.

Walker, Leonore. 1993. Battered women as defendants. In *Legal responses to wife assault: Current trends and evaluation,* edited by N. Z. Hilton. Newbury Park, CA: Sage Publications.

Watson, Sophie. 1990. The state of play: An introduction. In *Playing the state: Australian feminist inte rventions,* edited by S. Watson. London: Verso.

Weber, Max. 1958. Politics as a Vocation. In *From Max Weber: Essays in sociology,* edited by H. H. Gerth and C. Wright Mills. New York: Oxford University Press.

Williams, Patricia. 1991. *The alchemy of race and rights.* Cambridge: Harvard University Press.

Wollstonecraft, Mary. [1792] 1988. *A vindication of the rights of woman.* 2nd ed. Edited by C. Poston. New York: W.W. Norton & Co.

Yeager, Peter. 1995. Law, crime and inequality: The regulatory state. In *Crime and inequality,* edited by John Hagan and Ruth Peterson. Stanford, CA: Stanford University Press.

Yllö, Kersti and Michele Bograd, eds. 1988. *Feminist perspectives on wife abuse.* Newbury Park: Sage Publications.

Zerilli, Linda. 1994. *Signifying woman: Culture and chaos in Rousseau, Burke, and Mill.* Ithaca: Cornell University Press.

Zorza, Joan and Laurie Woods. 1994a. *Mandatory arrest: Problems and possibilites.* New York: National Organization for Women Legal Defense and Eduation Fund.

Zorza, Joan and Laurie Woods. 1994b. *Analysis and policy implications of the new domestic violence police studies.* New York: National Organization for Women Legal Defense and Eduation Fund.

Zorza, Joan. 1992. The criminal law of misdemeanor domestic violence, 1970–1990. *The Journal of Criminal Law and Criminology,* 83 (1): 46–72.